JESUS AND THE PAINT ON THE WALL

What Do People Live For?

JAIME MERA

i

Dedication

I dedicate this book to my beloved wife, children, and extended family. The hardships and joy we experience are best seen through our Lord Christ Jesus, who is grace and truth. God loves us and wants us to see and experience His love in His Son Jesus, not this world.

Contents

Introduction

❧ ----- ❦

I will start by making it clear that this book will offend some people and inspire others. However, it is your choice to allow yourself to be offended or not. Aside from that; have you ever wondered what it would be like to live in a piece of art? We all live against the wall, being forced around or enticed to follow things of this world. We see all the brilliant and dark colors in this world and call it life, while some people call it smelly stuff hitting the fan, then splattering all over the place. People live for many reasons, and most of the time they follow the painting on the wall, but there is something better. Jesus is our connection to live a life full of joy and righteousness, apart from this world. Jesus is not on the cross anymore, He is sitting on the right hand of God the Father, and He with us in the form of the Holy Spirit.

I will attack the status quo of main stream thinking about being politically correct, religion as a face of God, and what should be driving us to live without felling guilt or condemnation. I will talk about the belief that what you have heard or know about Jesus is true or completely different than what you believe. The scientific view of truth is analyzed not on a basis that what I say or other people say is true, but more what you know and understand as truth, false, or opinion which is tested by the scientific method. We must look at truth with scientific and spiritual vantage points. We must also see the truth as a constant and not something that is true today and is not true tomorrow without a reason for the change. I really don't want to get into semantics, so understand that there are many ways of saying the same thing; however, there are specific ways in which we understand a message because we are all unique with emotions, experiences, and beliefs.

You will notice that I will write in both objective and subjective tones, but I will try to make it clear of which tone I am using in a particular moment. There are many subjective viewpoints that people should not listen to because it leads to miscommunication and problems; however, there are viewpoints that should be considered even if it is subjective or even bias on special circumstances. It is extremely rare, but let me give you an example. You are a leader of a crisis action team assigned to conduct political negotiations with an African tribal state which have the potential to cause a mass murder/genocide situation or lasting peace between the neighboring tribes. You have a young and well educated man in the team which can quote you regulations, laws, and social negotiation skills. The young man tells you, in a very objective way, everything that sounds good to minimize problems when speaking with the tribal leader. You also have an older woman who has 25 years experience in negotiations and is an expert in this region's cultures and tribes. She personally hates the African tribal leader, but has never been unprofessional in her work and she tells you, she thinks and feels strongly in her gut that you should specifically confront the tribal leader with issues that caused the crisis action team to be deployed in the first place, and to lay out the plan for peace without being too appeasing, knowing the temperament of that particular tribal leader who sees appeasement as a sign of weakness. The dilemma is will you listen to a person because they are objective with sound recommendations, or do you listen to a subjective gut feeling recommendation which may have a better out come in the end, but may also have the worst outcome if the recommendation is wrong? You have to hear and understand the reasons for a subjective statement or idea before you disregard or accept information to be credible or useful.

What is said in this book should be looked at with a non-partial, unbiased, or logical mind set. Being politically correct or unclear with everyone is not my intent, and not being challenged by what this book talks about is you not having a stand on what you think you believe, or you are simply believing falsely. Long before the phrase not being politically correct was used, other phrases were used that went something like, he/she is uneducated, without discernment, ill mannered, not lady or gentleman like, or unsporting. However you may want to phrase it, being politically correct is only speaking without full use of vocabulary or context, and the verbiage should not cause you to close your mind to the message. An example of what I am talking about would be, if I say, "The movie is a piece of crap." Then the idea is that I am politically incorrect because I have said a bad word in or out of context where most people will shut out the opinion or professional critic because of the use of language. I submit to you, that if I had said, "The movie is a piece of poop!" Then I have said the same thing, but am more politically correct because it is said with a nicer/less offensive childish word which means exactly the same thing. People would say that I should use language that is befitting a neutral standpoint in grammar and idea by saying, "the movie is not worth watching and smells in all foul ways imaginable." There is no need to use slang or vulgar language in any instance to get a message across; which I will not do from now on, but there are many words that are not vulgar or slang, which are considered politically incorrect. Of course it is not just the use of bad language that makes things politically incorrect, but the meaning behind the word and intent are factors. If an African American, is talking to another African American and they both use the word nigger in their conversation, it might be acceptable or not acceptable depending on how each one is using it. If they are arguing with each other it might be their personal slang way of talking out of anger or accusations; but if they understand and accept the meaning of the word nigger as inappropriate, then they might not use the word because they want to speak in a more culturally accepted and modern time. Now, if a person who is not African American uses the word nigger or even sometimes the word black, in the presence of any African American or anyone for that matter it is an insult to the African American race and is inappropriate, which makes the words nigger and black politically incorrect. No matter what your view may be on wording, being politically correct is only a nice way of communicating, but a lack of politically correct words should not be the basis for not listening or understanding the intent of a message. Most of the words I will be referring to are religious in nature and should be viewed in context to what I will be stating or implying.

Please keep in mind while you read the chapters that the paint on the wall is all that this world offers and all that we accept from it. In reality, this world exists and we physically came to be in this world from birth, but our spirit is not from this world. Jesus is our true connection to a world which is yet to come and a new heaven which we will return to. I have purposely written certain examples or a list of descriptions. If you start reading and it seems to you like a random list, don't look at it that way. Look at the list and envision the description. I have mixed the opposites in those long descriptions, and it would help greatly if you imagine the differences among them, even though they might seem as the same occupation, belief, response, or descriptions throughout the chapters. An analysis of the human mind and habits will be looked at from a scientific viewpoint, a logical layman's viewpoint, and also from a biblical perspective. This book is for all of those who want to hear, for all of those who want to see, and for all of those who are tired of living a life of defeat, fear, hatred, condemnation, lost, or pride.

May this book be a great blessing to you and your loved ones, by the knowledge of Jesus Christ, our Lord and God.

Amen.

"In the beginning was the Word, and the Word was with God, and the Word was God."

John 1:1

"And the Word became flesh, and dwelt among us, and we beheld His glory, glory as the only begotten from the Father, full of grace and truth."

John 1:14

"He made Him who knew no sin to be sin on our behalf that we might become the righteousness of God in Him."

2 Corinthians 5:21

"and after he brought them out, he said, 'Sirs, what must I do to be saved?' And they said, 'Believe in the Lord Jesus, and you shall be saved, you and your household."

Acts 16:30-31

"that if you confess with your mouth Jesus as Lord, and believe in your heart that God raised Him from the dead, you shall be saved;"

Romans 10:9

Scriptures taken from the New American Standard Bible, 1990

True life lies in beholding and believing Jesus.

"and God said to Moses, 'I AM WHO I AM'; and He said, 'Thus you shall say to the sons of Israel, 'I AM has sent me to you.'"

Genesis 3:14

"The Jews therefore said to Him, 'You are not yet fifty years old, and have You seen Abraham?' Jesus said to them, 'Truly, truly, I say to you, before Abraham was born, I AM.'"

John 8:57-58

"I am the Alpha and the Omega, the first and the last, the beginning and the end."

Revelation 22:13

Scriptures taken from the New American Standard Bible, 1990

Chapter One

�� ----- ��

In The Beginning

(The age old question which is answered in many different forms)

Scientists, psychologists, theologians, and the average Jane or Bob have always asked who am I, or where did I come from? The father, mother, grandparent, or authority figure in that person's life would answer with a simple, "You are a human being, or a person, and/or you came from your mother." In some situations the person would say you came from heaven, a stork brought you to my window, I found you at the base of my front porch, or you came from outer space. Those people might be joking with the child or just avoiding having to explain what they think is an embarrassing explanation of child birth, or birds and the bees. In a God believing family, the parent will tell the child that they came from the mom and dad, but their spirit is from God. What we hold to be true is sort of subjective, but in reality it is subjective only to a person's opinion, and it is not subjective or a matter of opinion to creation itself. You as a person or living being exist, and feel life inside of you because you are, not because your opinion makes your existence a truth. So if you find out that the stork did not bring you to the home, then you must not be real, or the truth is not the stork story but something else. As for the reality of things around you, many people and creation witness to you about who you are and where you came from. As an evolutionist, creation follows the laws of evolution based on timed links of adaptation to the now present biological wonder of the union of a human egg and sperm into a developing baby of unique DNA arrangements. Other scientists have a similar if not exactly the same view as the evolutionist.

As a theologian, the premise of biology is the same for the present day baby, except that there are argued exceptions to the biological rule of a creation of a baby. The exception to the rule is in the written account of Adam and Eve, and birth of Jesus of Nazareth, Christ Jesus. In other non-Christian accounts, the exception is in the form of reincarnations, or human births because of Greek gods in heavenly places; other deities of many origins like Egypt, Assyrian, and Babylonian mythology that gave birth to the supposedly divine humans who for some reason all died or ascended into heaven for some future cause. In more radical realms of ideology, the exception is that aliens engineered the egg, so in this case the egg did come before the chicken. I did not list all possible accounts or will go into details on the birth accounts that say they are the exception, because they are not founded in hard consistent facts but are more in the realm of folktales. However, I will focus on the biblical account to this exception, because it has a very strong foundation of written documentation and consistent logic.

The biblical account of Adam and Eve is not to convince you that the first human who was created came from the earth in the ground, and that Eve, the second human, came from the side of the first human; but the account is more to show you what happened without having to prove it. Simply said, if you believe or don't believe the account it is not going to make the account true or not true, and does not take away the message that God wanted us to know and understand. Aside from believing as not being a deal breaker, the biblical account in Genesis shows us one thing which is not normally known or thought about. When God created man, He created the body from the Earth, molding him into Adam. Adam became alive when God breathed into Adam a spirit, which came from God Himself, not the Earth, not the ferments, or anywhere else except from God. God did not breathe into the animals of the world His Spirit. The spirit or life that we have comes from God's life or Holy Spirit, not just from the physical combination of complex cells to produce a body with a spirit. So, in this situation, Adam and Eve can say that they did not come from a physical mother. Jesus is also an exception because He did come from God and a virgin woman in accordance with biblical accounts of two gospels. So, Jesus did physically come from a mother, but not from a physical human earthy father. In essence Jesus as depicted in the bible came as God himself in the Spirit and joined with the seed of a woman to become flesh. Apart from Jesus we did come from the seed of both parents. However, even though you came from the egg and sperm of your mother and father; you have a consciousness which can reason and think. The life you feel inside of you which you can call your mind's consciousness, subconscious, or spirit came from God's essence.

Inside of you is a knowledge of who you are, and what you

think can affect how you interact with the world around you. This brings up the follow up question, "Where did I come from?" once again. The answers are multitudes of descriptions and facts. "I came from the south side, the Bronx, Miami, Mexico, Spain, midwest, a farm, a foster home, Delaware, Fiji, Beverly Hills, Italy, prison, Silicon valley, Paris, a refugee camp in Sudan, etc." The answer could be culture related; I came from a Mormon family, Christian family, a dysfunctional family, the Carrier tribe, the Cherokee tribe, or Muslim family. The identity of your family, whether born out of or adopted, is an identity that you grow up with and in almost all cases becomes the identity of you. Keep in mind that during your entire life you choice to side with or move away from your origin and initial identity. The identity can be due to genetics (race), family culture (ethnicity), or social community (varies from formal organizations to specific groups like a gang or cult). It can even be an affiliation in a family of police officers who identify with being a keeper of the peace, protector of life, liberty and property for the community. But the most of who you are; is what you have allied yourself to, and have incorporated into your character and life style.

At an early age you place trust into authority figures or emotionally stable figures like your mother and father. Not all parents show their compassion and many methods of discipline are factors for a child to view the world in specific ways. However, trust or lack of trust is the major mechanism a child uses to learn and incorporate an identity. Once that identity is established enough, trust is used to reinforce or change that identity. Teenagers who have not established a strong foundation of identity seem to have issues with who they are and what they need or should do in life. Sometimes it is because other teenagers, television, books, or mentors question or confuse the identity of that teenager. An example of this is, teenagers listening to drug use and hate music which is introduced by other teens or platforms. The identity of hate and doing drugs becomes a part of the teenager who has been taught that drugs are evil, but yet experimentation is okay according to other teens or adults. The dramatic display of people doing wild things on reality television teaches children and teens that certain behavior is either frown upon, desired, or tolerated. I will cover behavior when challenged with truth as an attempt to be accepted or evade punishment later in this book. So, there are a lot of what ifs and reasons for having bad habits and bad behavior. It is not really a question as to whether the behavior or habit is bad, it is more of a question of whether the person identifies with those bad or good habits and behaviors in a negative or positive way.

If a person is born in a community of families where cannibalism is a way of life, then the identity of the person will more than likely be that he/she is a cannibal and that eating human flesh is not a bad behavior. So, you might ask, who is to say that cannibalism is bad behavior. According to this particular community, it is not, and it is not illegal in accordance with the governing authorities in the region. The majority for most people is the authority to dictate what is right or wrong. This is a very arguable statement, because if the majority of the world thought it is good behavior to abuse your child and other children, then it is the authority of the people as a majority to say it is good practice, but does that make it good behavior? Unfortunately, the identity of a person is shaped by people who can in some misguided fashion be the majority who do not follow certain laws and ideas that were established in the past by God, kings, or whatever historical authority you care to accept. The Code of Hammurabi established a basis of laws for specific and implied bad behavior which is a part of almost all societies now in the form of laws and procedures for judging bad behavior and punishing that person for that behavior. An example is life in prison or the death sentence for murder or treason. The Ten Commandments set a base of not just proper behavior but moral behavior. These are general in nature, but the little things in life that a person uses to form an identity is a combination of where they came from, who is around them, what is influencing them to grow, and what is already established in the past.

So do you know who you are? Are you strong physically, mentally, or spiritually? Are you compassionate, happy, insensitive, always angry, envious, generous, unforgiving, weak, selfless, a quitter or a rebounder, or selfish? Are you prejudice or morally open minded but yet firm in good beliefs or even questionable beliefs? Are you a risk taker, or act due to fear? The positive thinkers are the people who know themselves and their identity in positive ways. The negative thinkers don't know who they are or if they think they do, they live in a world where their identity is to be negative. Have you seen people from all walks of life say, "It is the way life is?" "That is how it is done here," is also a common thing employees and employers say at work. "I don't have any money so I am poor." "I can't do that in a million years." "That is impossible." These statements are made by negative thinkers and a few positive thinkers who have started down that road of negative thinking. Positive thinkers on the other hand say, "How can we improve this job"; "I like to attempt the impossible"; "possible is my middle name;" or "I may be poor now, but I can only go up from here". I have never in my life heard the winner of any competition in professional sports say to the reporter after he/she was asked did you have any doubts you would win, say, "Yes, I thought I was a loser." No, the winner might say, "Yes, I was a little worried coming around the corner, but I pushed on and gave it all I had." The winner also would not say, "I had really big doubts and thought for sure that I was going to be dead last."

How you see yourself, dictates who you are. If you see yourself as a person without victory, you will find yourself in defeat. If you strongly identify with a culture, family, mentor, society, or way of living that empowers you with positive things, then more than likely you will know who you are and where you come from with strong conviction and understanding. If you accept negative things which also define who you are, it will produce the negative results you expect or don't expect. I will talk later about positive and negative aspects in life that not only shape your identity, but shape your actions and life as a whole. If you take any notion of identity as a part of who you are, or at least who you might want to be, it's a step forward in understanding and accepting what you live for in life. I will continue to talk about who you are in later chapters, but remember that the beginning of your life was not the end state of who you are suppose to be. You were not born a failure or even a success; you were born with life. What you do with that gift of life is up to you.

Chapter Two

ॐ ----- ॐ

Common Sense Goes a Long Way, If You Want It To

If a person is watching a television show, it would be common sense to reason that the person can see and is not completely blind; otherwise that person would not be watching the show, but maybe listening to it, unless that person were deaf too. If the color of a Giant Red Star is red, one would reason that the star is giving off a light spectrum that is seen in red. If a man values his life and is accidently standing in front of an oncoming truck knowing the truck will hurt or kill him, common sense would reason that the man will try or want to get out of the path of the truck, because he values his life and wants to continue to live. If a woman values her life, but for a selfless act of love and sacrifice she jumps on top of a grenade to save her children; common sense would say 'save yourself.' If she dies, then who will jump on the next grenade when her children are in the same situation? If she dies, who will feed the children if they have no other family to care for them? If she lives, she can have more children later and figure out how to keep another grenade from being in the scheme of her life again. Is this scenario a crazy unlikelihood? We will see.

According to Merriam-Webster dictionary (2012), common sense is, "sound and prudent judgment based on a simple perception of the situation or facts." Acts of valor, sacrifice, love, and many more strong emotions make things not so common and reasoning or perception of facts are usually measured in terms of a person's opinion based on experience, impulse, ignorance, or unwillingness to accept a situation or fact. So what makes things common sense or stupid reasoning, for a lack of a better word, is based on what you think and why, but there are other factors involved. I will start by asking, "Is common sense really prudent judgment??" In a community of people or group of people with no ties of mutual culture, common sense would be what the majority would say is sound logical reasoning that is based on a logical cause and effect type of action, or a state of existence. An example of a state of existence might be gravity. A car made out of metals, plastic, glass, rubber, oils, and leather is heavy because of gravity. Gravity and the car exist and act in accordance with the laws of nature. This is logical and can be argued to be scientific or prudent thinking. The same car in outer space has very little to no weight because there is no gravitational force strong enough to give it a heavy weight. Either way, the car has weight, whether it is 2,000 lbs or 0 lbs, it has a weight, but just a different description of that weight. The car can be weightless, light, heavy, or very heavy if the car could be placed on the surface of Jupiter. The interpretation of the state of existence, determines to a degree the interpretation of common sense. In other words, the car is heavy on the ground and weightless in space as common sense would reason because gravity exists and causes things to have a weight as the interpretation of what makes the car heavy or weightless in a certain environment. Another example is heat from fire. Common sense would reason that the intensity of heat from fire will burn a piece of paper. If the intensity can burn paper, it can also burn your skin, and so on. In essence, water or anything that has innate properties will have an effect that is consistent and innate themselves. Heat is hot, cold is cold, water is wet, sugar is sweet, a vacuum is airless, gravity pulls, and so on. This is a state of existence or state of being.

The cause and effect reasoning of common sense is similar. If the car is heavy and rolls over your bare foot, your foot will be injured. If the car is in outer space and is weightless, it would not be able to hurt you even if somehow your foot were caught between the car and another object of the same size as the car. The cause in this case would be the abundance or lack of gravity which determines the effect. Common sense would be that the effect was due to the cause every time. In the example of the mother who sacrifices herself for her children is in the realm of cause and effect. There is a problem though, because the cause for the mother was to save the children even though her death probably put the children to death anyways. The children will continue to travel through the war ridden country and be killed by another grenade tossed into a room, or maybe a land mine. She is not a stranger to war and common sense for the mother should have been to survive the war and have more children later. But is it really common sense? Who is to say that the mother's hope was not in vain? A hopeful and experienced war veteran who has lived a life full of near death experiences would say that the mother loved her children and reasoned in a split second out of hope that they would survive without her, as the hopeful veteran survived his entire life to an old age of a hundred. There have been miracles in history where common sense was not the path traveled, but yet marvelous things happened and people were saved or blessed. Likewise, there have been many disasters where a lack of common sense was the culprit.

I have a motto about common sense reasoning which many people would find to be logical, some people would find it to be impractical, and a few people would say it is obvious. The motto is, "If you don't want to be in the fire, don't jump in or anywhere near the pan." This is the basis of common sense reasoning. The people of Pompeii in 79 AD found out the hard way and died. The city of Pompeii was situated in the southwestern coastline of Italy near the modern city of Naples. They had a great and wonderful city full of all the best things in life they could imagine, but common sense would say, hey that volcano has been acting up in the past several months, it is an active volcano with a very recent history, and it is so close to the city. Maybe we should leave and move to Rome or go on vacation for a while. No, a lack of common sense became the reasoning factor because they did not want to leave the good life of Pompeii. They did not think it would be possible for the volcano to erupt, because that is what volcanoes do, right? So, once again, the idea that common sense reasoning would prevail was not common then, and it is not common now. Many people and livestock died in the Dust Bowl, in the central region of the United States of America in the 1930s. Many people migrated out of the area because they basically lost everything and common sense would dictate that the dust storms will eventually stop, but in the meantime, living in dust can be very hazardous to your health. The Dust Bowl lasted for about six years, plus they had a very bad rabbit infestation problem for a while too, but some people who survived and had reasons not to leave their land and homes, eventually prospered in their endeavor to be farmers or businesspeople. This example was highlighted because not all major natural disasters will automatically kill you, last a long time, or are common. However, there are common and reoccurring natural disasters which people all around the world face.

The natural events we see on the news are monthly if not weekly due to hurricanes in the Atlantic, typhoons in the Pacific, tornadoes in most states, earthquakes in many parts of the world, and major floods in low lying areas. So, common sense reasoning would say if you don't want a tornado to destroy your house, then don't get a house in an area where there is a high occurrence of tornados. If you have a house because it was given to you, then common sense would say to sell it and move. If you reasoned that moving is impractical because of family or job issues, then common sense reasoning would be to make sure you get a storm shelter built into your property. If you have had your house destroyed already, common sense would suggest you move or prepare to ride through another one. The people who complain that they can't believe a tornado came through and took their home on a trip to another county are going through what is called, denial. They might also be in denial because they never personally witnessed such devastation, but overall the idea that a tornado is no joke was never a doubt. So why is there a disparity of belief that a tragedy cannot happen to them? The lack of common sense reasoning is based on an unprepared mind or life style. Some people in Pompeii went through denial for a few seconds as they saw their own death unfold before them, while the fiery storm cloud hit the city. Even though there were many tall tale signs of imminent eruptions common sense reasoning was not used at the proper time.

There is a lot of common sense reasoning situations people run into everyday, but sometimes things are not practical. Many people have reasonable apprehensions for not moving or rebuilding the right way. Many people do not have the resources to rebuild properly, or move. But there are people who have the resources, but out of a fountain of hope and determination, whether spiritually or mentally driven, they chose to stay and live with the horrors of a tornado, hurricane, earthquake, and much more. Some people would say that common sense dictates that there is no place you can go where nature cannot get at you. There are people who move to specific areas around the world like northern Africa, or the Rocky Mountains even though there is a super volcano in the area, just so they can build a doomsday home or complex. Those are usually the people with financial resources.

But, what about those people who are not financially well off? What some people would say is impractical, can turn into a do or die situation. Barbarians in the 1st through 14th centuries have fallen into this category. The Gaul tribes decided to migrate from the northern regions of what is known as Romania and Ukraine, south into Rome controlled lands, because they reasoned that the Mongolian army was on its way to kill them or conquer them in the 1st and 2nd century. The fact is that instead of fighting the Moguls, they ran away as a race and ended up fighting against the Roman Empire later down the road. The Saxons who were living in the northern coastlines from Germany to France moved away from the coast, because mass flooding was so bad that they were forced to move inland. Common sense became subjective, because the reasoning for moving was due to acts of force, not with any real voluntary choice to stay because it meant probable death to stay and fight, or stay and drown. In most cases however, people don't listen to common sense, and let the world dictate their decisions even though they are not in a life or death situation.

Many people moved to different lands looking for fortunes, freedom of religion, fame, or running away from something. Common sense would say that moving should be based on the most logical and beneficial course of action for the person or loved ones. This is basically taking an educated guess as to what the future might hold for deciding things like moving. Some people would say it is trying to find greener grass on the other side of the hill. Many people suffered hardships in the westward migration in pursuit of gold during the California gold rush of 1848. A little more than a quarter of a million people flocked into the west to find gold. Only a few of those gold hunters made it rich, while the other people either died in the attempt, or returned to their home with about the same amount of resources or less than what they started out with. I am sure there were people who had very little to lose, so going off on a gold finding mission might have been using common sense reasoning. The reality is that they did not think about the hardships, they thought about the little that they thought they had and the wealth that could replace their own present life. I am not saying that the majority of the people did not have or use common sense thinking, what I am saying is that practical reasoning is not just based on logic, but on taking a well educated leap of faith. Taking a chance and hoping that all will be in your favor, not because you know better, or have a lucky or psychic hunch; but because you have looked at the cause and effect and taken the path which seems to best suit yourself and others. For the most part, people do reason things out and use common sense, but what about those people who don't?

The people you see on television or read in the newspaper that break into places like gas stations, try to escape the police, blatantly lie saying they are not drunk while falling flat on their face, jump head first into a dark pool of water not knowing how deep it is, or smoking next to highly flammable barrels of gasoline on a factory floor. There are many more most shocking and dumb things that people do, but is it just a lack of common sense reasoning? I also attribute the aftermath of a lack of common sense reasoning or wisdom to these peoples' moronic behavior. A simple example is when a police officer stops you and you pull over to the side of the road. You are in hurry and are late for a very important meeting with the possibility of losing tens of thousands of dollars. Your employer is not going to be happy and you could possibly lose your job. You have not been drinking, but you did go over the speed limit by maybe eight miles per hour. The morning fog is a little heavy, but you can see at least 100 feet in front of you.

The police officer takes his time and comes up close to your window. "Good morning Sir/Ma'am, can I see your driver's license and registration?" he says with a calm and friendly tone.

You are frustrated and look at him with an angry gaze, and ask, "What did I do wrong?"

"Sir/Ma'am, you didn't do anything wrong," he tries to explain.

But you cut him off in the middle of the explanation saying, "If I didn't do anything wrong, then why did you freaking stop me? Today is a deal breaker for me at work and I might lose my job because of you wasting my time and yours."

The officer looks at you a little agitated but keeps his cool. "Sir/Ma'am, your brake lights don't work, and your tags are expired. Please wait in your car, I will be back." He goes back to his squad car to fill out a citation and takes his sweet time about it.

You on the other hand forget about common sense and get angrier the longer the officer stays inside the car. You get so out of control that you get out of your car to find out what is taking so long.

The officer sees you and on the speaker tells you to get back into your car.

You ignore the police officer and what happens next is that the officer goes through a trained drill which is meant to keep the officer and others safe from hostile intentions or accidents. The officer gets out of his own car, keeping the car door open as a shield, and either pulls out his weapon or is ready to pull out his weapon. He points at you with his finger to get your visual attention, and loudly commands you to stop and get back into your car, or tells you to stop where you are and place your hands on top of your head or the roof of your car.

What will continue to ensue is a chain of time consuming events which will get you into more trouble simply because you didn't listen to the first common sense reasoning situation and acted out of anger or whatever other emotion or person you might care to blame.

Common sense would dictate that even if you are prejudice of the police to include a gender or race that the police officer may be, that cooperating with the officer's instructions will give you a faster and better outcome. Cooperating includes speaking in a friendly manner, even if you feel like breaking something. You could have started by deciding to listen to the officer and accept whatever reason the officer stopped you for, accept the ticket and go to work and then deal with the ticket later.

If you would have kept your cool, you would have noticed that the officer was more concerned about your break lights not working with the heavy fog being a high risk for an accident. If you nicely told him that you understand the break light issue, and that you were going to a very important meeting that could cause you to lose your job; depending on the distance, the officer might have escorted you to the job site. It is not likely, but you never know when you will be blessed, and if anything, the officer would not have taken his time with writing the citation or warning. The faster you got moving the sooner you would have gotten to work.

In addition, you now know that your break lights are not working so now you can drive being careful not to stop all of the sudden, or at least put the emergency blinkers on.

If for some reason you don't listen to common sense at first, there is still hope. The officer can go back to his squad car, while you go through anger management relaxation exercises knowing that you need to keep your cool or the officer will only delay you more than normal. You call work and let them know you are tied up in traffic and give them a location so that at least the boss can decide whether to change the schedule a bit for the meeting. There are many positive possibilities and courses of action that people can take if you use common sense and don't burn bridges.

It is not easy for people who have had their entire life, ripped out from under them, and then decide to rebuild there once again. Common sense would dictate that they move somewhere with less problems. Common sense, would also say that if you do decide to stay, to rebuild so that you can survive again and possibly savage or protect more personal things the second time around. Common sense is not used very offend, especially if a person uses really bad excuses, like they need money to support a bad habit, addiction, or the family. If you start to think about robbing a gas station, common sense would say that not robbing the station and getting a job would be better. Common sense would also say, as a well known saying goes, "If you don't want to do the time, don't do the crime." If you think you will cross a dark highway full of moving cars without looking to see if the coast is clear and expect everyone to stop for you, then you are not using common sense. If you think that experimenting with drugs, shoplifting, lying to your parents, lying to your spouse, eating unhealthy foods, and many more negative things, do not have consequences, then you are not using common sense. If you don't want the consequences, then don't do something to start the ball rolling. If you are already in the middle of the consequences, there is still hope. Common sense can prevail, if you want to change your circumstances without getting into more trouble.

What you decide on a daily basis will not go well with you if common sense reasoning is thrown out of the window, and you continue to accept the life you have as perfect or that is the way life is. Common sense reasoning is based on wisdom which incorporates preventive measures in almost all cases. Wisdom is defined as, "the quality of having experience, knowledge, and good judgment; the quality of being wise (Dictionary.com, 2012)." Experience and knowledge is a key to good preparation. An example is if you are going to drink alcohol, then the first thing reasoning would ask is do you really need to drink? The second would be if you don't need to, but you want to, then other things arise. Are you legally old enough to drink, are you taking medication that will cause problems with the introduction of alcohol. Do you have to drive after you finish drinking? Are there people around you that you can trust with your possible drunk condition later? Do you know the dangers of drinking alcohol? Do you understand responsible and irresponsible drinking habits? Have you researched alcohol related issues that can contribute to spiking of your drink, scams to rob you, or behavior which can lead to sexually transmitted diseases? Can you trust someone to be a designated driver? Awareness is a factor in common sense reasoning. Unlike the definition of common sense with prudent judgment, awareness is basically how you perceive things but not really understand things. We are taught in school, say no to drugs, and we are educated about the bad things about drug abuse and the good things about proper medication. Whether we listen to wisdom or not at that age is another story. We are also taught at an older age to don't drink and drive, have a designed driver, and most recently, drink responsibly. All of these ideas are preventive measures, but like my motto recommends, 'don't get in a position where bad things can happen to you', hence common sense reasoning would say, 'drink water or a maybe a protein shake.'

But the fact is that people want to experience what they think is fun. Until the day they go through hell in rehab, see a loved one go through rehab or out of their minds, see a loved one dying from lung cancer or related illness due to smoking, alcohol, or other drugs. Common sense reasoning is a logical way of thinking, a process which tells you how to stay out of possible trouble, and helps you while you are in the midst of a problem. Understanding common sense reasoning as a state of existence, and cause and effect, goes a long way if you allow it to. Also, understand that it is not a one day transformation. Looking at Jesus and receiving wisdom is the basis of perfect common sense reasoning. Wisdom as the person of Jesus, not some way of thinking or living. Wisdom is what will keep you out of trouble, or get you through it with a peace in your heart. The first thing God gave to us was wisdom through Jesus, in 1 Corinthians 1:30, "but by His doing you are in Christ Jesus, who became to us wisdom from God, and righteousness and sanctification, and redemption (NASB, 1990)." Looking at, learning about, and hearing about Jesus will supply that wisdom and much more for our lives on a daily basis, not just when we most need a miracle.

Chapter Three

❧ ----- ❧

Problems or Opportunities

Everybody has problems. It is said that some people have more problems than others. Now if that is true then I want to know who is keeping count. Every day has its own problems. For some elementary and high school students, the problems start with getting up, making your bed, maybe taking a shower, eating, or getting homework finished that was not finished the night before. It could be finding the perfect clothes that make you look cool in school. It could be doing early chores so that he/she can go to work after school. It could be many problems before school, but what about the rest of the day? While in school, it could be fifty to a hundred math test problems or a science project. It could be getting through the day without being bullied. It could be getting through the day without being embarrassed from a weak bladder or accident. After school, it could be doing chores, staying out of trouble, or sleeping early. For the parents, it could be things from child rearing, to working, housekeeping, communicating with the spouse, alcoholism, drug abuse, spouse abuse, child abuse, unfaithfulness, pornography, debt collectors, homelessness, a flood in the basement, a death in the family, taking care of a sick pet, a terminal illness, a chronic illness, a mental disorder, confinement, or simply said, surviving the day in the most comfortable way possible. So what are the problems which I am really talking about? The everyday harmless problems that are a part of everyday tasks are not the problems I am talking about. I am talking about the problems which can harm or cause other problems that can harm you or other people in a direct or indirect way.

A habit, usually a bad habit, can become one of these problems, but I will address habits in a later chapter, so my focus is identifying a problem and understanding that problems have solutions. If a problem did not have a solution, then it would not be called a problem, but a fact which cannot be changed. What people tend to do with problems that seem unsolvable is give up and accept the way life is, or do things which only create more problems. I know of and have heard teachers say, "This kid will never learn or grow up to be anything worthwhile." This has been said about bullies, kids with flunking grades, and special education kids who need an effort by the teacher and parent to teach them. Their solution, both educators and sometimes parents, is to just label them as un-trainable, unreachable, or failures. This is where ignorance, a lack of common sense, and a desire to continue with the status quo come into play to make a problem seem unsolvable.

Another harmful problem which can affect people in a negative and harmful way is being an alcoholic. Common sense reasoning would dictate that drinking alcohol for the first time, drinking underage, or socially is not a good thing if you don't know your limits or don't have a plan to be responsible.

Ignorance comes into play when you don't know all the facts about alcohol, you ignore the knowledge others have experienced, or you have an attitude like you drink because others are doing it. Understand that many if not all alcoholics saw it coming, but were blind to the disease because they had other problems in life, liked the buzz, or wanted to use alcohol to replace other bad habits. Once the alcoholic accepts his/her condition as a problem, it will be possible to get that person to fix the problem because the person does not want to continue in the status quo. If the person fights the healing process, it is because the person is fighting the hardship involved with fixing the problem or in fact the person has not really in their heart wanted to stop the status quo. This is simplistic because an effective support system makes all the difference for an addict to be successful. Everyone is different, but there are many people who have succeeded in overcoming or solving problems, because of the support system they are willing to follow.

These people had a desire to change their situation, a plan whether it was theirs or someone else's – like interventions, and they had support in the form of people, visuals, audio, or physical tools. These people for the most part have an attitude of positive thinking, or are being influenced by a positive outside force if they think negatively. You see this in many support groups for people trying to get into shape, stop smoking, prepare for a GED at an age of over thirty, getting rid of an addiction, and much more. The attitudes are not just positive, but they are attitudes with an expectation that even if the goal is not met, life is still good. It is an attitude of persistence, patience, and confidence. Persistence and patience is easy to understand; however, I am talking about a confidence not in you but in the situation. Confidence that what is before the person is not a problem, but an opportunity to make things better than before. Confidence to know that not all bad things last forever. Confidence to know that all is not lost, that every problem has a good solution. Confidence that you are not alone, and if you feel alone, it is because you are not paying attention to things around you, to include God or whatever spiritual being you care to believe in. Confidence to know that there is someone that cares, even if you can't see them or know them. Confidence to know that God can and does work all good and bad things for your good.

The people who are depressed, down trodden, have low self-esteem, or feel condemned are those without this confidence. They are normally the negative thinkers or do not have the positive support group or influence around them. If you go to a home where the children are told they are worthless, brainless, inept, a waste of a life, or a street brat; you will see that the children do not see themselves in a positive way. This negativity most of the time keeps the children stuck in their problems. When they grow up to an age when they can leave home, or if they run away, the negative attitude that they were taught compounds the existing problems. If they do not think they can achieve higher things then they will accept the status quo and live a life of mediocrity. By looking at problems as opportunities people can have confidence to try to change the situation. Granted, that problem solving skills taught in school, at home, on many social networks, games, and the like, help people get confidence in fixing problems. But this is just more than practicing problem solving skills; it is a confidence that anything is possible. Problem solving skills can be separate from the person's knowledge and experience. An example of this is when a young child is given a puzzle for the very first time and the child has no idea on how to put the puzzle together, or even that it is suppose to be put together. An adult will put the puzzle together showing the child, and then introduce a different puzzle. The young child will in time be able to put a brand new puzzle together without any further assistance or prompting.

If we look at all problems in a similar fashion we will look at the problem as a new puzzle and an opportunity to put the puzzle together without the assistance or instruction from someone else or have any idea of how to solve it, but we can try. Mind you, good quality assistance should never be turned down, but it is the attitude which will drive you to see solutions in the making, instead of problems. Whatever, your mind set is at this point, it really does not matter. You can change if you want, or involuntary on rare occasions, but hopefully for the better. It is possible to have a positive attitude and then all of the sudden a tragic event happens and your attitude changes to a negative and defeated mind set. This can happen as fast as a few minutes. Some people have had strong religious beliefs, and once they lose all their money or their entire family is killed in some accident, they denounce God or whatever deity they were worshipping. Not that their convictions and beliefs are weak or false, but that their confidence and trust is not being reinforced by results. However, there is what is called an attitude of not problems but opportunities. In the book of Job, an Old Testament account of where Satan asked God for permission to bring tragedies into Job's life to prove that his faith in God was false. Job's daughters and sons were all killed in a span of a day by what some people would call a freak of nature or an act of God. Job praised God instead of cursing Him even though he had lost his family and home. Satan then inflicted bodily harm on Job's skin with stinking blisters in all crakes of his body. He had lost his family except for his wife, who was trying to motivate him to denounce God, while his property, children, and health were attacked. Job had three true friends who came to his aid, they did not motivate Job to denounce God, but they did not witness of God's faithfulness and goodness. It was not until Job prayed for his friends to be forgiven for their lack of praise for God that God fixed Job's problems. Not only did God give Job his health back, but He blessed Job with double the number of daughters and sons. God doubled Job's wealth and property. Nothing was said about the wife afterwards and his friends were blessed because of Job's faithfulness and patience. Now what does this all mean?

In many sermons by preachers, many messages have come about from this event. But I am not here to tell you the moral of the story, I want to direct you to the fact that Job did not look at his tragic problems with a defeated negative attitude, he looked at his problems as an opportunity not for him to fix, but for God to show him a miracle and His faithfulness. Many motivational speakers and preachers who preach grace talk about what to look at. You can think that having a sprain foot is a problem, or as those speakers would say, at least you have a foot. There are many people who wish they had feet but are in wheel chairs or use prosthetics. You can appreciate things better if you can see what not having feels like, and be thankful for what you already have to include being alive. Many people are beaten down by passive or negative thinking which has infiltrated into all areas of our lives to include the church.

This attitude towards problems as opportunities is not the only thing you will need to achieve success. So far you have read about knowing your identity, and common sense reasoning. There are a few more things which will help you in being a positive thinker with firm problem solving skills and convictions. It could be scientific in nature, psychological, spiritual, or instinctive when looking at the white lining of a cloud. The consistency of seeing the positive side of life among all the paint on the wall will give you the confidence to take on whatever major problems come your way. It is easy sometimes to say every problem can be fixed, but I must point out that there are people who have life threatening problems. Many people are presently dealing with a terminal illness or are victims of evil plots or tragedies, where hope seems like a meaningless word. If you say to that person, "this is not a problem, it is an opportunity," he/she will want to repeatedly hit you with a baseball bat. People, who are at this stage in life with that kind of problem or problems need to hear encouragement in the form of empathy and I am here for you; not just simply to hear someone say you need to change the way you think. I will address what Jesus has done for us in a later chapter, but there is real immediate hope, even in the face of death. This attitude about problems being opportunities is for preparation and daily living, not for first time usage when a crisis occurs, or for trying to encourage someone who does not think the same way at the time due to the emotional pain that person may be going through.

One last thing that needs to be addressed is that

confidence is best experienced when you understand that the righteousness of Jesus gives you right standing with God the Father. There is no problem that God cannot get you through. You don't need a mediator to have Jesus work for you, listen to you, or be your source to draw from. You do not need to fall on you face and beg for forgiveness so God can help you. Jesus would say to you, don't be afraid, and embrace you with His love. The righteousness which Jesus has attained on your behave is yours through Him and only Him. If you have asked Jesus to be your Lord and Savior, you have this confidence that Jesus is personally working for you, and if Jesus (God almighty) is for you, who or what can be against you?

Chapter Four

ॐ ----- ॐ

What Defines You

We talked about knowing your identity, but there is more to the story. Who are you now? Are you the one who cries while watching a romance movie, a tragedy, or any moving moment in life that causes you to see what is good, honorable, sad, or some injustice? Are you the one who cheers when you see something righteous, the bad guy getting caught, the underdog winning, a woman or man stripping, or a person getting beat up? Do you get angry at everyone for not following the rules, not leaving you alone, not paying you due money, stealing money from you, disagreeing with your ideas, or doing something unrighteous? Do you have a sense of humor that everyone seems to accept because you do not use vulgarity, like Bill Cosby? Do you have a sense of humor that is ironic or sarcastic, but not everyone is comfortable with? Do you empathize with people, or do you expect others to naturally feel what you feel? Do you demand perfection, or accept honest mistakes? Do you have an ego that is selfish, or simply confident with room for others? Do you lie on purpose, or do you lie because you cannot accept the truth? Do you stand for truth, even if it means pain in your life? Do you wish the best for everyone, even if a person is behaving in a despicable way? Do you forgive others, or only those that you think deserve it? Do you demand forgiveness or do you want to be forgiven? Do you condemn those that you feel should not be forgiven, and be put to death as quickly as possible so others will not be harmed? Do you have a sociable personality, or are you a loner? Do you see life with hope or are you a pessimist that expects the world to end in a horrible ball of fire?

It should be easy for you to see that how you see things is also how you are. If you see yourself in your heart as brave, you will more than likely be brave in times of great distress. If you see yourself as fearful and worrying about everything, you will more than likely be afraid to act in a time of great distress. If for some reason you have a mask where you show people that you are happy and nice, but inside you are sad and bitter; then you are not living how you see yourself. It is not natural to live contrary to your feelings and self image, and for the most part people do live their life the way they see themselves. The people that do not are usually consistent hypocrites in positions of influence, con-artists looking to deceive people, or people who define themselves by negative aspects of causing harm to others, thieving intentions, selfish intentions, or simply confused, allowing the world to bash them around like popcorn in a popcorn machine. I am not talking about actors who get paid to show a character that is completely different than their real personality. I am not talking about pretending in a game which is played by toddlers up to the elderly with role playing games, plays, or scripts. I am not talking about the confused person who doesn't know who he/she is and is trying to find an identity. I am talking about a person who has an identity, but willfully puts up a facade because he/she does not want people to know the real identity he/she has adopted.

Most people who do this feel condemned or are in denial of condemnation. This condemnation is due to the many negative influences around us, and also due to what is known as the law. Whether you believe in God's laws, nature's laws, or legal laws, all of them tell you that if you break the law, you have missed the mark and there is a consequence which is usually followed up by punishment. Why am I talking about the law and not who you are? Well they are interrelated no matter how much we admit it or not. We all live somewhere, and there is a governing authority telling you that killing someone outside of self defense in against the law, stealing, raping, and many more offenses are punishable under an established criminal justice system. The punishment could be confinement, death, a monetary fine, cutting off of a hand, restriction from another person, deportation to another country, or a combination of many creative punishments. We all have or had authority figures like our parents, who also have laws in the home and outside the home until you get to a certain age. Even then the laws are enforced by the owner of the house and apply to all who dwell or visit there. In school there are regulations and laws as well. Everyone knows the laws because they have been taught the laws or they just know in their heart that something is right or wrong. The identity which you adopt is tailored to these laws. In effect, because of these laws you to some degree punish yourself when you do not keep the law. This is what people call a guilty conscious. It is also called self condemnation. Now, there are people who seem cold with a heart of ice, who don't care about moral laws and kill, rape, and torture other people for laughs or whatever warped reason they might have. These types of people have adopted their identity to apathy and several other negative things. The law is still there in their heart whether they care to admit it or not. The proof is in this, if the person did not feel that what he/she was doing was wrong, then there is no reason to hide it or evade police; except that they know immediate punishment and judgment by other people is part of the consequence for being open with their crime. Legal laws in the world are not the same as the laws God placed in your heart, but overall a person knows when they do wrong.

For the people who do seem to have a conscious and don't go on killing sprees or similar illegal activity, they too have the law in them whether they admit it or not. What makes the difference between a people that is not self condemning himself/herself with one that is, is more than scientific. It is not just thinking that you are or are not breaking the law. It is not being accepted that can make you feel condemnation. All people who have been raped, abused in any fashion, or humiliated by people, especially by people they trusted have felt self condemnation. It is not the person's fault that the evil incident occurred, but due to whatever psychological or spiritual reason they almost always blame themselves to a certain degree. This blaming business is of course one of those negative influences that push a person into a negative definition of themselves, usually unwillingly. Therapy and programs help a person cope with and recover from the damaging effects of this self-condemnation, but it takes more than psychological exercises to accept who you are and accept the good inside of you. You have an ocean of emotions inside of you and your thinking interacts with those emotions. How you see the world around you, how you see yourself, and who you think you are play into these emotions. The laws which you have ignored as much as possible, tried to follow, or broke them because they were already broken only complicates things because we end up living our lives constantly trying to follow or break all the rules. This conflict between what you want to be, what you should do, and what you actually do is what helps or hammers in defining you. Maturity is measured in how you manage this conflict between emotions, your adopted identity, what you actually do (how you follow the rules), and who you want to be.

Everyone wants to be someone, even if it is not to change who you already are. We get asked in school or at home at an early age or in college, who do you want to be or what do you want to do when you grow up? The answer varies from a doctor to actor, pilot, firefighter, President of a country, teacher, Spiderman, Tarzan, architect, lawyer, interior designer, and much more. However, I have yet to hear someone say I want to be a fast food attendant or portable toilet cleaner. These occupations or titles are not glamorous and have not been praised as something a person should strive for. They are necessary in this world and I am sure that if kids are taught in school that these occupations are important and positive in many ways, one child will want to do those jobs when they grow up. Whether it will be life fulfilling or not is another issue. What we strive to become is usually a person, a personality, or an ideal. An ideal like Superman, or Wonder Woman who are strong, super intelligent, and fight for justice. A personality like; Sam in Quantum Leap, the Doctor in Dr Who, or the always happy and caring nurse in the hospital. A person like a big brother/sister, mom/dad, favorite teacher, or mentor. Unfortunately, what many people want to be in certain periods of their life is to become the idol they dream about; usually, celebrities like an actor or actress, athlete, singer, or even a criminal. Everyone has a choice, and you can want to be a good person, a man/woman of God, a fighter for justice, and many more positive things. Or, you can want to be a lazy person, selfish person, a loser, or many more negative things.

I am bringing this example to show you attitudes and how people are defined by their thought, belief, and action. The four marines who were, caught on video, urinating on Afghani citizens in January of 2012, was a reflection of what defined them, but was it really their actions that defined them or their character which was seen by their actions. I am sure that the criminal investigations all focused on seeking the truth and punishing the wrong doers. But what is the truth. Were the dead bodies of civilians or terrorist? Did the marines witness their fellow Soldiers die in the recent past because of terrorist insurgents as those in the video? Well to be frank, all that doesn't matter. It could have been a thousand terrorists who just raped and killed each marine's daughter, wife, mother, or sister. It could very well be innocent civilians or terrorist. It doesn't matter. The reasons for and actions of the Soldiers were wrong in all possible ways, whether the Soldiers believed they were in the right or not. First, whenever a Soldier or any citizen travels to another country, that person is whether they want to or not, a representative of their home country. The Soldiers are representatives of the United

States and the US military who stand for life, liberty, the pursuit of happiness, and justice for all; in the sense that they fight for our freedoms. Second, they all have given their oath, their word, that they will follow the orders of the leaders appointed over them, and that goes up to the President of the United States as Commander and Chief. I am sure that President Obama did not order down the line for the Soldiers to behave in an unbecoming manner. In most places in history the word of a man was his assurance that he was not lying. Well if you look at this, lying is and will always be against moral law, or at the very least wrong.

Looking at the incident from another perspective, there are many people who if the situation were reversed, the terrorists would be urinating on bodies of dead Soldiers; but as before, that does not excuse the behavior. This is another indication that the Soldiers were acting on adopted identifications of negative ideas self justification, hatred, and others that were in their minds. Third, what possible satisfaction can come about their actions and what logic is there in getting caught on video? This is an indication that common sense reasoning was not there and it was replaced with an identification of thinking they were justified. Lastly, each one of them did not have a defined character to do what was right, even though they had military training.

This concept of doing what was right hinges on a matter of discipline, stress, and coping mechanisms which the marines did not use or control. You can be a strong willed, a perfect leader, a perfect manager, have all your 'T's crossed, but in a day of constant pressure, and unique circumstances, the leader can make a bad decision, have a nervous breakdown, or follow the wrong path. Discipline is something everyone can more or less relate to, but when there is a lack of discipline, there is chaos. At one point in time before that particular day there was a breakdown in discipline and the marines forgot about their identity as representatives, or they did not have that identity reinforced in them to begin with. Either way, this is not an acceptable reason for a collective behavior by four supposedly disciplined Soldiers. People all have faults; however, as any person with responsibilities in a job, if you are negligent, incompetent, or simply do not work to standard, you will be fired, legally prosecuted, or retrained. People are expected to do a job well in which they were trained in. The people that do well are the ones who have identified themselves with a good work ethic, fulfilled accomplishment, honor, have pride in their work, and a few more acolytes. The people who identify with laziness, unethical practices, or self serving goals are the ones who don't do their jobs right or pay attention to details.

I am retired from the US Army and have personally seen thousands of men and women serve their country in a very honorable and selfless manner. I have also seen many of these Soldiers with problems like any other person on the street. There is a difference however. Almost all military personnel have a drive to be competitive, fight for the values we hold dear in our free society, and have a very adaptive mind set. They are trained to solve problems in war and to act quickly and efficiently. They have this can do attitude and they do act the fool sometimes in a social environment like any other person who parties on a Friday night, but are not inclined to be recklessly criminal. There are however, those Soldiers who have adopted negative things and they do commit crimes and do really dumb things. But I submit to you, if those marines had defined themselves as a good person without condemnation, then they probably would not have committed that act. I personally would have looked at it this way: if they were dead terrorists, then they should be buried like any other person who died. If they were innocent civilians, then they deserve my prayers for their families who are still alive, and if possible have the bodies transported to be buried in accordance with their families' wishes. I do not think I am better than anyone else, but I do define myself from a holy perspective and things that I do can bless people. I am not the Apostle Paul, but imagine the possibilities from a perspective in biblical accounts of the Apostle Paul. The Apostle Paul was so anointed by God that the clothes he wore could touch someone and they were instantly healed without him having to be laying hands on them. Now imagine if the Apostle Paul was there next to the Soldiers. Well once spoke or dropped a handkerchief from his pocket on the dead bodies they probably would have come back to life, which would be a very good thing for the now living people. Obviously that did not happen and the Apostle Paul would not have behaved as the marines, because that is not what defines him. There are many preachers now and in the past, like Smith Wigglesworth, that have raised the dead or healed people of terminal illnesses, just like the Apostle Paul.

The attitude of these people was not one to go and urinate on people or send a message of hatred, and I guarantee that they are conscious of their behavior and what they do because they are defined by who they are, what they do, and what they expect from themselves in Christ Jesus, not the world. They do not see themselves condemned, a slave to the law, or to negative thinking;

they see themselves and believe that they are righteous by the blood of Jesus, blessed, and think positively. If you ask a born again Christian, who understands grace and truth, "What defines you?" He/she will tell you, "Jesus defines me." Understand that what defines you is not your actions alone, it is your core beliefs and how you think/reason. That definition will come out and be seen in your actions.

So, what else defines you to have these core beliefs: a good reasoning process, a good upbringing, a good mentor, or a good example? Well all of these have merit with each other. In the military, everyone has a direct supervisor or they are a supervisor. The leaders are taught to lead by example and the subordinates are trained to follow and become a leader. As leaders we are also trained by learning or reinforcing values of morality, honor, duty, respect, commitment, courage, and quite a few more. We are told we are expected to be trustworthy and full of integrity. We are in many ways being told that we are good people and focus on the positive. Unfortunately, not all Soldiers are exposed to a constant barrage of: you are the best of the best, you have integrity, you have compassion, and you are a disciplined Soldier who knows what right looks like, and so on. The minimum amount of time a Soldier gets to serve their country is two years, and there is plenty of time to not receive that constant positive reinforcement. Somewhere in a person's life, negative things and negative thinking gets into a person's identity and the positive takes a step back. This happens in the military, at work, in the home and school. If you ask any educator old enough who has been through the school system back in the 1930s until now can tell you the major changes in how students treat each other and what they are taught about themselves. Depending on where you live, in the 1970s and 1980s, there were no gang fights or weapons found in most schools. Now a day, the violence and lack of values in school has exploded compared to the past. It is the lack of training in the school, at home, and in society that has given the student and now adult the values which have and will continue to define who you are, starting by what you think and believe which will come out in your actions. Media has contributed greatly in exposing negative thinking and negative social behavior to young viewers. But, it is not the media alone who is at fault, but the world in general and the people who follow the world. The past cannot be changed, but the now is what matters. It always helps to want to be a person with values, a righteous character, and all those things we see as good. But once you have figured out what positively defines you, and who you are, just simply be yourself.

The actions which you show on the outside will be what you have already on the inside. If you don't like what you see, maybe you should look deep inside of you, and decide to change, and adopt positive defining influences. There are some factors that will help you in times of confusion or condemnation. Once again the factor or people or things telling you that you are worthless can affect you slowly or swiftly. "Sticks and stones can break my bones, but words will never hurt me," is a classic saying and is for the most part consistently true only for those who understand it. It is true to the person who knows this, but not to the child or person who accepts words as true which allow for verbal abuse. A child who is ignorant or trusting of an authority figure who is abusive gets these negative ideas inside their core identity. Words have many powerful effects, and can harm you or heal you. The influences of words are part of who you are, but positive words for some reason tend to work better only if followed by results.

Many people turn towards religion, mental science, or medical science for those positive influences if they do not have idols, people or examples to follow. Unfortunately, what people search for and find is not always what it is claiming to be, but is in fact a temporary fix or false. Advertising on television for quick fixes for losing weight, getting rid of wrinkles, unwanted hair, and much more are examples of what people get attracted to in an attempt to change their look and who they are on the outside. There is nothing wrong with wanting to improve yourself, but just like there are money scams in things for the outside, there are scams for the inside too. When you see a 10-Step method for improving your mind to stop smoking, for only $9.99, then you should beware of what may define you if you grab at things that may or may not work. The attempt to change your character or habits is commendable, but easy fixes that end up not working give you a sense that results are not being met and your character ends up thinking negatively. The term buyer beware should be applied to words and ideas being sold to you which can define your thinking in positive and negative ways. Associations to people or so called friends also sell you a bag of good and bad influences. Everyone is different and unfortunately people accept words and ideas according to those differences which can be good or bad. What defines you can be people, ideals, words, or life experiences, but what brings all those things together is what we call choice and your heart.

The heart of the well known Tin Man in the Wizard of Oz was a heart of strength, mind, and courage. A compassion or warmth which knew the origin of love was motivated to always do the right thing. In an opposite view point a broken heart is full of sorrow and despair. The heart of a person is said to be the body, mind, and soul, the center of a person's essence. The book of Proverbs 23:6-7 says, "Do not eat the bread of a selfish man, or desire his delicacies; for as he thinks within himself (*reckons in his soul*), so he is. He says to you, 'Eat and drink!' But his heart is not with you." The context of these two verses talk about how your thoughts within your soul are also who you are or will be in your heart. Many people use terms to describe a person's core identity, like a heart of gold. This term is not far off from an identity which is centered on a person full of righteousness because gold represents righteousness in the bible, and a few more things not necessarily biblically related like healing, blessings, faith, wealth, or power of a king or Supreme Being. An identity which is engraved in your heart will help guide you in life. This is why it is important to understand what defines you. If your heart is full of bitterness, hate, fear, condemnation, and many more negative things, then your identity will be those things. Something that will help you in your path to define who you are is that Jesus has given you freedom from condemnation and all those other negative things, which means that in your heart there is peace and all that we see as true and good is there through God's gift, His Son. Jesus has given you a heart of pure gold, but for some reason people don't use it, like the Tin Man before he met Dorothy Gale.

Chapter Five

❧ ----- ❧

Religion Is Only a Word
People Use

Religion has many meanings according to several different dictionaries. One definition in accordance to Wikipedia online, "Religion is a collection of cultural systems, belief systems, and worldviews that establishes symbols that relate humanity to spirituality and, sometimes, to moral values." Another set of definitions in accordance with Random House dictionary: Religion is a set of beliefs concerning the cause, nature, and purpose of the universe, especially when considered as the creation of a superhuman agency or agencies, usually involving devotional and ritual observances, and often containing a moral code governing the conduct of human affairs. The second definition is a specific fundamental set of beliefs and practices generally agreed upon by a number of persons or sects like the Christian religion or the Buddhist religion. A third definition is the body of persons adhering to a particular set of beliefs and practices like a world council of religions. I have given you these definitions to help explain that there is a difference between what we call religion, a denomination, being a Christian, the person of Jesus, and a belief or way of life.

People use the word religion or religious for many reasons besides what the definitions above state. The word religiously is used to describe the intensity of a man hunt, a diet, and many more meticulous endeavors. The word religion is used to describe not only a way of life but a hobby or sport, like surfing is my religion. Scientology and other systems of beliefs are called a religion, whether they are acknowledged by the established authority or not. The word religion is used as and has been demonstrated for a myriad of things to include ideas, but what are we really suppose to see or understand when the word is used.

Looking at comparisons or differences might help in clarifying why I say that religion is only a word people use. I will start with the difference between religion and denomination? A denomination is a branch of any religious group, but is mostly attributed to the Judeo-Christian church. Every denomination has a set of unique dogma and focus which distinguishes them from each other. This is why you have Baptists and their kind, Protestants and their kind, Methodist and their kind, and a few more. The word denomination is normally not misused or misunderstood to be a special word attributed to one single belief system alone. I did not include Mormonism, and Jehovah Witness, because they do not stop at the bible, but have their own version of a bible or holy works. In other words they do not follow the Old or New Testament Biblical accounts. They are not branches; they are their own 'religion'. You are probably saying to yourself, how subjective and prejudice is this guy. Why am I only focused on the Holy Bible? Well in order to understand the person of Jesus you need to look at the source which claims his person, while other religions do not claim the person of Jesus, they all claim God or Allah, but Jesus they only claim him to be a great prophet.

I also did not include the person of Mohammed, Buddha, or other figures because they do not represent what Jesus represents, by their own claims. Many preachers of grace teach that Jesus is not a religion; that grace is not a thing, but that grace and truth is a person. I will explain this statement. If I were to tell you about the great Rev. Martin Luther King Jr. and who he was, what great things he did, his day by day life story, what would you say about Rev. King? He preached about God and freedom to live in a place where there was no prejudice and hate. Would people name a religion after his name? Maybe, maybe not. If I told you a great story about Mohandas Karamchand Gandhi on whom he was, what he did, what he taught, and the great things he advocated, what would you say about him? Now what if I told you I was a follower of Mr. Gandhi and started a church in his name. Have I made a religion? Possibly, but let's step back. What exactly were all those people in and around Israel, to include the disciples of Jesus, doing after Jesus was crucified, was raised from the dead, ascended back to heaven, and the Holy Spirit on Pentecost came to the believers? The people who were later labeled as Christians where not talking about a religion, they were talking about Jesus. They spread the word of who Jesus was, what He did, and what He is doing, because He is alive now. They used the Old Testament and their own testimony, which turned into the New Testament, which talks about Jesus. The Old Testament witnesses of Jesus in shadows, types, and direct references; his first coming; his victory over sin and eternal death for us; and His second coming. The New Testament also witnesses of Jesus, starting from the beginning, what He did for us, His love for us, and His second coming. The good news, the gospels speak of Jesus and His kingdom; Jesus as a person and God in one. People have made the word religion to cover all of the ideas which we see as spiritual entities and cultures, but in reality the good news of Jesus is not a way of life or belief system, it is a witness about Him. The fact that Jesus has included us in His victory, in His person, in His eternal life - is the good news, and not what we think is a faith in a book because we only see a set of rules, have faith and God will be or is real because religion says so.

Well, you don't have to believe me because I say so, go and do the research. There is more and more witnessing now in these last days talking about Jesus, not religion. We are in a generation called the Benjamin generation, where people are witnessing to the grace of God in Jesus' righteousness in us and for us. We have heard so many people saying repent, repent, judgment day is coming and we equate that to a religion, because we hear the words God, Jesus, or revelation. Unfortunately, many people are stuck in this idea of religion, and do not see that Jesus is our Savior and Lord, not a word we call religion. So what does this have to do with you? The world has been painted in our lives for us to see and experience on a wall like in an art gallery. The world we live in is physical, biological, metaphysical, and cosmic for a lack of more descriptive words. There are those who do not believe in God, but they do believe in something else like science, Mother Nature, super beings from outer space or that we are alone on Earth for the moment. There are those that believe that

God exists, but the god they believe in is not the God of the Bible, but some other aberration. So, why did I give you this lecture? Whether you believe in God or not is not what I want you to focus on. The fact is that the world exists and you are living in it right now. How you live in this world is for another chapter in focusing on Jesus so that your life will be more abundant. What I am saying is that when you hear the word religion; do not assume it is talking about the definitions in the introduction of this chapter or that the usage of the word is done in context and correct. Jesus is separate from the world and what we call religion, which is from the world.

There are many more words which are treated the same way and are completely misused like imperialist, capitalist, socialist, conservative, or liberal. The best way to see the misuse is to look at the author (is the author being objective, bias or subjective), the context, and the logic of the statement. An example is a statement that I have seen a lot in newspapers, propaganda, and books. The statement goes in various forms but to summarize, it is in reference to the United States as an imperialistic regime with no respect for other countries. Well the use of imperialism is by far a misuse of the word in meaning and in context. An imperial regime is one that uses force to govern, has direct governing power over an entity, and is ruled by an emperor or single ruler. The Random House dictionary has imperialism as the policy of extending the rule or authority of an empire or nation over foreign countries, or of acquiring and holding colonies and dependencies. Unfortunately, people have equated this policy to the USA, of which Spain, England, France, and a few more have practiced in the past and controlled other nations, states, and nation states.

I submit to you that if in fact the US was an imperialist nation state, then the US having to rule means they should have the authority to legally judge and persecute citizens of another country in that country. For instance, if I were a South Korean citizen, the US would have the power to step into the Korean court system and put me in a US court system and punish or release me without cause or permission from the South Korean government. This is the same with all nations where the US has an established military foothold. In addition, the foothold is there because that country has asked for the presence or is in agreement that the presence is to be in the best interest of the country. I am not talking about a country which has been invaded due to issues like a war; attempt to stop genocide, or a collective effort to defeat terrorism or the like. Even then, the US does not dictate the judicial or social system within that country for their citizens. I have not even touched on the fact that the allied countries which have a military presence can tell the US presence to leave. The fact is that those countries don't want the US to leave for economic, political, or militaristic reasons that benefit them or their neighboring nations. Britain is the only country that I can think of that has most reflected the definition of imperialistic actions in 20th century; this was demonstrated by their enforcement of rule in the Falkland Islands. People use the word imperialist like drinking water when the US flexes their military and political might, even though it is not to impose rule. It is extremely rare to hear someone call the late Soviet Union, Germany, Iran, or Italy in the 20th century as imperialist because they tried or did take over many countries at that time by force and did impose their rule on the citizens, trumping the established government. Oh, I forgot to mention the back and forth invasions of Israel and surrounding nations, Greece and Turkey, and of course the Mongol empire, Rome Empire, and a few more. I understand that people try to use the word imperialism to describe US foreign policy and actions as a kind of police force in the world, but they should use other words and descriptions to better communicate their meaning of the activity or idea.

Another example is if it is related to a Holy War, then the word infidel is used instead of imperialists. The author who uses words out of meaning and context is to blame, but the reader must understand and beware not to accept a word to mean what the author says it does because it is used in a sentence. When it comes to answering questions of who am I, what defines me, and what does life have for me, you should keep an open mind to understand words and the use of words in their context; in particular, religious, scientific and the other non-religious words that relate to you.

Chapter Six

৯০ ----- ৫

Science Verses Psyche

Science is always trying to be objective, with measurable observations, or collectable data. Science is a way of life for many people and if not for science we would continue to live in a world of who knows what. Science has been around for a very long time, maybe as far back as can be recorded, even in biblical accounts. Farming which is a form of science was first mentioned in the book of Genesis. It is important to note that you don't have to call something science or be a scientist to prove something is founded on science. Science is according to the World English dictionary: the systematic study of the nature and behavior of the material and physical universe, based on observation, experiment, and measurement, and the formulation of laws to describe these facts in general terms. It is also known as skill or technique. Farming is not something that anyone can do, and it is very scientific in nature with respect to weather, chemical reactions, geology, entomology, and a few more 'ologies' which can grow perfectly engineered grapes or a barren field of depleted top soil. We have accepted farming to be a hard science in that there is no real human or emotional factor that will change physical observations like psychology. Science is very specific and many young people have suffered long hours of studying, homework, and experiments only to find out that measured observations cannot be seen in the world of love or psychological science. Or can they?

Psychology has gone a long way since dad let go of the bicycle and pretended to be holding it as Jimmy or Susan rode his/her bike down the sidewalk with a big grin on his/her face. Today, there are student interventions in school and at home which are specific for all kinds of teens, special education children, and what is called as regular class students. The interventions are adaptive to individual students and are measured by observed behavioral changes or improved performance on tests. Science has developed personality tests, individual evaluation plans, intervention workshops, small group workshops, and many more psychological based tools. The term social-emotional learning has been a focus for educators today, because it has been effective in teaching students as a collective. Small group workshops using the Jigsaw or Student Teams-Achievement Divisions (STAD) strategies have evolved into the classroom, which is a welcomed improvement from corporal punishment teaching or lecture methods in the past. The social-emotional model tells us that we are social and emotional beings who interact and learn/grow by this interaction. Science has been able to measure to a point the behavior when we interact, and this includes when it comes to our emotions like love, but our psyche is a different story.

The Radom House dictionary says psyche is the human soul, spirit, or mind. However, the word psyche refers to only the soul in other sources, which is derived from the Greek language. Soul and spirit are separated in meaning or context from other standpoints. The spirit of man is always referred in the bible as the immaterial part of man. Man is not a spirit, he has a spirit. The soul (psyche) is just what the Greek word implies - the makeup of man, which can refer to the essence of a man that makes man a man/female. It is sort of confusing because the words interact with each other in literature. But mind is a little easier to separate from the concept of soul and spirit. Science explains the mind as a neurological process of synapses in the brain that communicate with the body to form ideas, decisions, commands, answers, and questions. That is the logical way of explaining how things work in the mind, but I am not here to talk about the accuracy of how we see the psyche in one or three parts. The psyche is where your desires and needs are realized or revealed.

Science which also relates to culture tells you that you are an adult, man, or woman by hitting a specific age, passing puberty, making your first kill on a hunting trip, or legally attaining a state of competency by the way you can support yourself. The problem is that both science and the psyche says that adulthood is attained by the full development of your mind and maturity based on how you think and your actions. Many people over the age of 20 act like childish spoiled brats sometimes, while there are very responsible and caring children who act like grown adults at times. Science would say that juvenile behavior is due to many situational circumstances and biological influences, while adult behavior is a combination of situations and experienced character. In essence, science says that knowledge along with cause and effect is the reason for behaviors. The psyche says that the mind behaves on its own, but takes what it wants or needs into account.

Unfortunately, many people do not distinguish the difference between what they need and what they want. You hear advertisements all the time about how you need to buy a brand new car, a dream home, a revolutionary cutting knife or frying pan, and many more, 'you needs.' But do you really need these things? If you have a reliable car that gets you to where you want to go with no major issues, why would you need the same car but newer? We are taught early in life to know the difference between needs and wants. Your mom and dad would tell you we need to pay the bills or we will not have electricity, a house, or water today. Your mom or dad would tell you things like I want to take you to a movie, or ask you if you want to go eat ice cream. The interaction of everyday life teaches you needs and wants. However, when there are mixed messages like in the advertisements, people get taught that wants and needs are the same. The psyche is fooled, but science is not. The reality in life which science embraces is simple math. When a person cannot buy a roll of toilet paper because math says there is not enough money, that person understands that he needs to get enough money to get the needed toilet paper, or find another way. Yes, the person might want something like food; but in a desert, the person also needs food and water to survive. So in a way the advertisements were correct and both wants and needs can be the same. This only confuses a person and then what happens is that emotions get mixed in with logic/science and vice versa. We end up fighting both or taking a side of science or the psyche and get nowhere close to use them both as we should.

So, what does all this have to do with science and psyche? Science being knowledge and logic, while psyche being mind, soul, or spirit with sometimes chaos and no logic, in fact complement each other. Science does not fight against the psyche. People try to explain the mysteries in the world or unexplained manifestations like in the television show called Ghost Hunters. The already assumed to be real spirit of a person is the focus of scientific investigation with specialized machines and experts to show observable proof of the spirit(s). Psychics are used to fill-in the blanks or confirm criminal investigation methods which are scientific in nature, known as criminology. Magicians use sleight of hand to fool your psyche in emotions while scientifically you are fooled physically. The big fight which people seem to think exists is the fight between science and the spirit, in this case what people mean is science verses religion or things of the spirit. Science can measure love, hope, faith, humility, hate, apathy, and many more psyche related things or ideas, but there are limitations. Some people would say science can measure those emotions or values in the form of visible behavior or feelings. If a woman is day dreaming with a wide smile and singing, because of a man she just met or has been dating, science would say she is in love because there is active chemistry at work in her or both of them. They may end up getting married until death, or split up after a year or two, when the chemistry has died down or another cause and effect changes the measure of love between them. So to some degree, love was measured. However, when someone says that God loves you, science says either God does not exist or the person is reacting to an ideal which makes him/her feel love sensations or affirmations. The psyche would say, "Should I accept this or should I go with my feelings, logic, or have faith (trust) in that God loves me?" I have not covered all the viewpoints covering a measure of love between two people or a person and the spirit of God.

The thing is that science is based on what is seen, mixed in with human psyche which can be emotional, subjective, and illogical at times. People didn't question the assertions Aristotle had about falling objects due to gravity and was not proven to be wrong until 1,900 years later when Galileo Galilei performed experiments with measurable observations and repeatable results of objects with different weights, dropped from the same height, fall at the same speed, which contradicted Aristotle's assertions that heavier objects fall faster. Other people might have said Aristotle was wrong, but Galileo was the one to show it in writing with the help of science. Now, during those 1,900 years, what Aristotle said was accepted as the scientific law of its time, but yet it was flawed. The psyche is the same way, especially with the ideas of many people who have been wrong and right. The balance which should be between science and the psyche is taken to unbalanced levels when people want to just see one side of the human spirit or the scientific order of the universe. There is another aspect that people do not see. Science is inherently question based and the results are more questions. Matters of God are not question based, they are answer based. God tells you the answer, not a question for you to figure out. Whether you believe the answer is another issue in itself.

There are things which science cannot explain and people should accept that we cannot understand the full extent of the spirit because Jesus, the creator of everything that exists, is above science and the world we inhabit. It is like if we are two dimensional objects on a piece of paper with no height and only depth and width. We will have no understanding of height, just distance across one end of the paper to the other side. No matter how much we want to see height if we theorized it somehow we could only probably imagine height, but never see it. A three dimensional being understands height, width, and depth; and understands a two dimensional being's world. An article published in Discover magazine by Lanza and Berman (2009) talks about this concept. They said, "The only thing we can perceive are our perceptions. In other words, consciousness is the matrix upon which the cosmos is apprehended. Color, sound, temperature, and the like exist only as perceptions in our head, not as absolute essences. In the broadest sense, we cannot be sure of an outside universe at all." Now, imagine that a two dimensional being had a psyche where faith is required to believe that there is height. That being was given that psyche and told there was height by another being who was in reality a three dimensional being who put his footprint in the two dimensional world. The two dimensional being could imagine the other world, but he will never see it or understand it with science, and he will have to rely on what the soul, mind, and spirit can only give.

The psyche allows us to have an understanding that defies the visual aspects of a universe that has laws and limitations which the spirit does not have. Science has come up with many theories to explain creation, the universe, or the psyche we all have. There is the Big Bang Theory, Infinite Universe Theory, and Theta-MEST of which the Big Bang Theory is the one most commonly accepted by the public and scientific community as the most credible of the three. Evolution and a few other theories have also been science led and achieved a hierarchy of importance as facts/theories. Note that theories are considered facts or theories which are proven false. So the leading theories are considered facts which are supported by test after test or find after find. However, not all theories are true like the example of Aristotle and gravity. There are theories about the spirit, but in accordance with all we presently know there are limits due to our knowledge and technology. So what have I just told you? I said that science and psyche do not fight each other; but at the same time, they cannot at this point explain everything we want to know because they have limitations and different ways of working. The psyche works on a spiritual and mental level, while science works in levels of the physical universe (physical representing all aspects of science).

There is another aspect of life that people would view as scientific or spiritual or both. Aspects of balance or an equilibrium of nature that are both scientific and spiritual according to many beliefs. Voodoo for example, is based on good and bad forces where a balance of the forces is required to have true health or peace. The Yin and Yang is also a polar opposites trying to work together to establish a balance. They are not a balance in the sense that peace and joy is the balance, but more like the negative forces are not the dominate influence and hence the balance is achieved. There are problems with these views however, because from a scientific viewpoint the balance would be considered in many ways a compromise and neutral. In essence true paradise is not possible because there is always a negative side. It also contradicts or fights against the idea that the negative is a part of life, so that if there was not hate, then love would not exist, or better yet, there has to be hate for love to be revealed. Now, Yin and Yang do not view it that way and see that hate would be a natural opposite of love and there is no contradiction. The laws of science say that there has to be an opposite reaction to any action.

Now all this seems to makes sense in a logical way, so if we look at it through a world which was perfect in the past and is now infected with imperfection, we can go further. If we look at it with the idea that there is evil and good, then there is also a knowledge of good and evil, which has a resemblance of beliefs of balance and laws of science. People have heard of angels and demons (fallen angels), or of forces which basically represent good versus evil. Science has its limitations because the spirit world sort of speaking cannot see or explain what was not there before creation of the universe, like love, good and evil. The spirit can tell us, but it is limited to our perception and by what force evil or good we listen to. There are many things involved with perceiving a spirit led life, but in a simplistic way, if the spirit inside of you is troubled, it is because it is more than likely not from a good spirit in particular God's spirit. Jesus gave us His peace, so when you are being led and walk the way He wants you to go, then it is His peace you will feel. There will be things we cannot explain and won't be able to for a very long time if not ever. We must accept or understand that there are limitations, and knowing this can better help us understand ourselves and the world we live in, but are not permanent residents of. We should use and not ignore both science and the psyche.

Chapter Seven

ॐ ----- ॐ

Thinking and Habits

Many problems, beliefs, habits, and behavior is the direct influence of what we think, but before I go any further, I want to say something that Joseph Prince has preached many times; that right thinking produces right living, and wrong thinking produces wrong living. I have talked about what defines you and the behavior you demonstrate is due to the character which defines you on the inside. How you see yourself also gives you motivation to be positive or negative. To add to this list; what you think is important to you also dictates how you live your life, how you think, and what habits you adopt into your life. If you place importance on drinking coffee, you will make a habit of drinking coffee every day. If you place importance in making money you will probably end up devoting more time on making money than other things of less importance to you. If you do not place importance in going on vacation once or twice a year, you will probably not go on vacation unless someone makes you go, like a significant other, or children. This also works on your beliefs. If you place importance on a specific belief, you will probably attend a temple, church, synagogue, or assembly on a regular basis. If you place importance on a person or topic, you will probably study about the person or topic and use that information to define yourself. Now, to what degree of importance you place on things is another factor in how much will be adopted into your thinking and habits.

You probably have heard people say, "You need to prioritize your life." This statement is heard in school and at work with a twist to prioritize your daily schedule to be able to study better, or prioritize tasks so the work can be completed on time. Milestones are created and checklists are used to keep track of things which have to be done. Usually, checklists only organize and manage schedules by timeline, not really by importance. Milestones focus on importance of things to be done, but also show timelines. In a material world, milestones and checklists are a great way to be organized at home, school, and work. People who have mastered these management skills continue to use written menus, schedules, checklists, and milestones to maintain a clean and tidy house, but there are those who have the prioritized lists in their head. They have kept the house or worked in their profession for so long and have everything programmed into their routine without the need of a written list. They have for the most part made the priority list as part of a habit for them. They do not have to think about it, they just do what they know at the same time and with the same effort every time. This is a conditioned habit. People who have done something over and over to the point where they do it without mentally questioning themselves all the time can be considered a habit, but that is not true by definition. A habit is a settled or regular tendency or practice, esp. one that is hard to give up, according to Webster's dictionary. Factory workers do redundant things which they do not think twice about, and they may have reflexes at home when they perform the same movements as if they were at work because they are in the habit of moving a certain way at work. This type of habit is not what I will talk about. I am talking about habits that a person has which define their character and life style. I am not talking about an addiction, but habits can contribute to maintain or get rid of an addiction.

Habit is not a bad word; there are good habits and bad habits. I was told that you can stop smoking by replacing your bad habit with a good habit. They were partially right, but like I said an addiction is not a habit in of itself. This is why many people have problems with getting rid of an addiction which they classify as a bad habit. You cannot get out of alcoholism by replacing your alcoholic habits by changing to non-alcoholic beverages and that is it. There is pleasure and unpleasant aspects of the alcohol, but the motion of drinking is the habit, and the disease of the addicting substance is not a habit, it is a disease which biologically and emotionally permeates into the body and the mind to reinforce the habitual motions. The habits we will focus on are the habits which we live with on a social and emotional level that are not addictions. When we eat foods that we like, we tend to eat them because they have the sweets, sours, saltiness, bitterness, spiciness, or greasiness that are in essence substances that our bodies react to. They are not addictions, they are pleasures or disgust that we tend to repeatedly want, or stay away from. It can become an addiction due to the chemicals in the food, but a majority of the addiction is psychologically motivated. People, who severely struggle in eating moderate portions, eating at proper times, and staying away from sugar, too much carbohydrates, bad cholesterol, or sodium, usually have unproductive eating habits. People who bite their nails or fidget too much usually have emotional behavior reasons behind them, but the action of the habit is one that subconsciously tells them that they are meeting a need. But like food, the need is not really a need, but a desire for satisfaction, pleasure, or whatever psychological reason the habit is performed. The end result of the habit is what makes it bad or good. A good habit could be always checking to turn off electrical things before you leave the house. A bad habit can also be just leaving the house and not checking to see if the space heater was turned off, because you are in the habit of just leaving the house. Why is there a difference in action that makes them a good or bad habit? As I said earlier, the amount of importance you place on something makes you think and act in specific ways. If you understand and place importance in making sure you minimize the possibility of an electrical fire or just to conserve energy, then the satisfaction or pleasure in accomplishing this task is fulfilled when you check and turn everything off. If you don't care about reducing a possible risk for a fire or you want the pleasure or convenience of being lazy out of ignorance, then the habit of just leaving comes easy. However, habits are either replaced with good habits, get worse, or they are forced out of practice. An example of being forced out of a habit is when a person has a bad habit of always talking back to superiors or authority figures. In the military that habit is quickly stomped on with threatening commands, precision disciplinary measures to jack up the person or else he/she will be punished under judicial authority and power. In like fashion, a person who is found guilty of a crime, the prisoner is disciplined to the point of solitary confinement or if the inmates are involved, you are forced to submit in many unpleasant manners. So, some habits are broken by force, or actually replaced by fear or desire not to receive displeasure. If we talk back to a police officer or a parent the things which follow are not pleasant and habits tend to be changed. There are people who speak in a vulgar manner which they picked up with a group of workers or friends, but once they socialize with a family member whom they haven't seen for a while, they are quickly corrected in the language use by a slap on the head, or a lecture by mom, dad, grandma, or sibling. The embarrassment of your vulgar language usage in front of someone who is part of the family, trusted friend or a person of demonstrated moral values is the factor in changing the habit. At that point, the amount of importance you place in listening to your family and following the rules outweigh the importance of you continuing to speaking vulgarity. But what do you do when there is a habit that is not broken due to force? If it's a good habit, keep it, if it's a bad habit; decide if you want the bad consequences to continue to occur now or in the future.

There are several key things that normally happen when you decide that a bad habit is not for you. The person first must want to change, otherwise the change will not occur or it will only be temporary. Second, the person must have a plan to solve the problem and get results. There has to be a constant motivator for the person to completely execute the plan. If the plan is too complex or takes a lot of determination and there is no effective support, it will probably fail. Many successful methods of execution, resolution systems, or teaching methods are those that keep things as simple as possible. In addition, if the plan is flawed like a worthless medication program to lose weight, or an expensive step by step program that only works for a specific situation, then the change will not last, if there is any change at all. This is why people tend to go back to biting their teeth, speaking vulgarity when things go wrong, or gain all the weight that was lost. There is no support system to maintain good behavior or habit that replaced the bad habit. In addition, the negative things which can define us is always attacking our good habits or reinforcing our bad habits. The support system can also work against you. Most parents have seen this when their children get involved with what is called a bad influence in the form of troublesome friends, illegal activity, sex out of wedlock, and a few more. The support is a negative type of support where the best method in changing the bad habits is to get the person away from the negative support system. This is easier said than done, because if the person does not want to change the habits, he/she will not want to separate from the negative support system.

Either way, the person has to want to change a bad habit or be forced to change. A desire to change is great, and hopefully there is a good plan available with a good positive support system on your side. Now, being forced to change is not all bad. I gave an example earlier of prison forcing you to change a habit, but there are other things that change you which are not as bad, but not pleasant either. If you have a habit of leaving a convertible car with the top down all the time and one day you come out and find it soaking wet inside because of the rain; you will make it a point to change the habit or end up ruining the inside of your car every month. If you have a habit of oversleeping, when you get a job that requires you to get up early, you may not have the job for long if you oversleep habitually. Once you lose the job which may be important to you or not, you will either change your habit or keep the habit and get a job where you don't have to wake up early. Either way, the experience of losing a job or having to find another job because of your habit may be enough to force you to change it. Now changing a habit can be unpleasant, but that is where common sense reasoning should come in and you compare to see which one will give you the best results short term and long term. If a bad habit is truly bad, then the bad habit should always lose in the comparison. What people have a tendency of doing with some bad habits is only look at the short term and weigh the pros and cons. The problem with this is that it is sometimes easier to maintain a bad habit which does no immediate damage, then to put time and effort in changing it. A good example is exercising and eating right to not just lose weight, but to get and stay healthy. The person has a good support group at the beginning, but it becomes a hassle to go to the gym or do all the exercises and then eat small portions of food being always conscious of food choices. It is a hassle because the person is not used to the program and has probably wrong expectations of results that are not being realized. The person goes into this let me stay the way I am because it is easier to accept my situation and ignore the negative comments made by other people and nutritionists. Until the day comes when a heart attack is experienced, high blood pressure is the cause of many problems, or diabetes becomes a problem. All because the long term expectations were not met in the short term period. Unfortunately, the person will not look back at the work he/she elected not to do in the past for preventive purposes, but looks at the here and now. The person will change some habits, and deal with the consequences, or continue to look at the easy road most traveled because that in itself has become a habit for this person.

Long term reasoning should be a major factor in all decisions to change a habit. Many people who were forced or strongly motivated to change, thank God or whoever assisted them in the end. The results are realized and then they see that the efforts were worth it. But, what about those people who try and try only to find themselves picking up more bad habits or increasing the frequency of a bad habit. These are the people who seem not to be able to get an effective program/plan, support system, or they are not thinking in a proper way. These are the people for example that may lose some weight and gain it back a few weeks later. Gaining or losing weight is not a habit, but the habits which cause this weight gain or loss is what people want to change, they just describe it as losing weight. They try another program and lose weight again, then gain it all back with some extra pounds a few weeks later. They live this roller coaster life until something gives. The person will change something that allows them to keep the weight off, or the person just gives up and stops trying to lose weight. In some cases the roller coaster effect or substances that are used to lose weight physically or mentally damage the person. Some diets work on depletion of certain nutrients which can be counterproductive to a person with or without medical conditions. It is also possible for a person to get burnt out if exercise and diet is improperly conducted. So how can this type of roller coaster problem be resolved before it becomes a roller coaster? The way you think and how you accept or reject things once again comes into play.

The all but true positive thinking attitude will motivate you constantly to be determined to the end and never quit. The idea that all you need is to think in a good determined way is of course not all you need. The importance you have towards something helps in organizing and putting the amount of thought into your actions, but that also is not enough to get out of a roller coaster situation. You have to accept that failure or not getting to a particular goal is not the end of the world and it is not your fault. Sometimes even if you failed because it was your fault that you didn't follow the instructions or kept doing wrong instead of listening to your inner self, you have to look at it as a brand new start and not your fault. Condemnation does really bad things to your thinking, and believe it or not, guilt is easily accepted by people because we all have grown up with laws which we have all broken. I am not saying we all have broken one or a thousand laws, what I am saying is we have broken at least one, and that is all we need to have broken to feel condemnation. How you might ask? If a child is taught the basic of laws, do not lie, do not hurt or kill any other person, do not steal, be nice to your siblings, don't go anywhere outside the house without my permission, don't interrupt people while others are speaking, don't talk back to your mom or dad, and many more laws, that child will at one point break at least one. Even if it was by accident, the child will know that the law was broken. I don't call these laws as rules if you noticed. Rules are for organization and guidance, while laws are for knowing what is right and wrong, or good and evil. We have swimming pool rules so people will be safe, not so that people will know if something was wrong or right. People on many occasions however, interpret pool rules as law and they fear punishment because right/good conduct brings blessings or praise, while wrong/evil conduct brings curses or punishment. Newton's third law of motion states basically that an action on an object produces an equal opposing reaction. In a similar way, an action produces a consequence, whether good or bad. The difference is that the reaction may be less or more depending on other influences. So in the case of the swimming pool rules, there might be punishment in the form of not being allowed to enter the pool for a time period, or a deep scrape and scars on both knees because the person was running and fell. Both of these are consequences, but the fact that the person thinks they broke a law is what matters in our thinking.

Condemnation is even more powerful when we condemn ourselves, whether justified or not. There is good news though, and it lies in ways of forgiving, understanding what condemnation is, and knowing that Jesus has taken away all condemnation from our lives forever. If I told the people at the swimming pool that if they try to follow the rules and even if they break a rule that was posted on the wall, that they will still be allowed to swim as long as they ask for forgiveness and try not to do it again. Do you think anyone will feel self condemned for breaking a rule? Some might feel more condemned than others, but they all will still feel condemned to a point because asking for forgiveness is now part of a requirement or rule. It does not mean that the requirement for forgiveness is a right or wrong, but people tend to see it that way. If I don't forgive, I will not be forgiven is one of those requirements we accept as law and also has been misinterpreted, but in reality is wisdom trying to show you that if anyone has a right not to forgive you it is that person you have not forgiven, so you should forgive because you have been forgiven. But the most wonderful thing about all this condemnation and law business is that Jesus has taken our punishment upon Himself and gives us His victory which is eternal. He fulfilled the law for us and took the punishment of eternal death for us on the cross as a sacrifice to God the Father who judged us in Jesus. We cannot be condemned because we are not being judged anymore in this world if we accept Jesus as our Lord and Savior, what we are doing is fighting a lie that we are being judged for the believers, and for the unbelievers they are still under the law because they have not accepted (believed) Jesus' finished work.

So, do you have to believe what I have said about Jesus? Not really, you can try to follow the law and continue to fight condemnation. Some people will succeed to a point and think positively because the condemnation which they saw they were able to manage or overcome. The thinking process of not giving up, not feeling condemned and using common sense reasoning will work for an unbeliever, or even for a believer, but the best way is to understand that condemnation should not be in the equation at all because Jesus took it all away to include the law. Believers who understand righteousness through Jesus, and grace and truth, have an advantage in following the law or rules, simply because they want to, not because they think they have to. An example of this is trying to keep the commandant of thou shall not commit adultery. They don't commit adultery not because the law says it is bad, they don't commit adultery because they love their spouse and are not worried about being condemned. They don't think about being condemned, they think positively because they are free of the law.

Positive thinking and good habits, they both interact, but what if I told you that both are useless if life seems to pass by with no purpose or sense of fulfillment in your life. The roller coaster ride and other bad habits are part of your life, and they are only a small section of challenges which intermix with an unfulfilling or fulfilling life. The life which we should all be embracing is the life which Jesus offers and gives us. Focusing on Jesus gives us the power to rest in Him, and allows His Spirit to work in us and for us.

Chapter Eight

꙳ ----- ꙳

Seeing What Right Looks Like

Seeing what right looks like is a key to doing what is right and living a life of success. Life is so much easier when you have a supportive family, school mates, mentors, and teachers. Supportive in the sense that they understand your dreams, goals, and desires in life. They want the best for you and they take every chance they get to help you in life. Grandparents and parents give all they have in money, advise, instruction, time, and several other emotional and physical things so that the child can fulfill those goals and dreams. In many cases, it is also the dreams and goals that the parents want for their children, like becoming a well educated, compassionate, and independent man or woman. But it is also not so easy in life when you don't have the support system and all it takes is for one out of many people or things to mess things up.

I will start with family. Parents who push their children into straight 'A's, a mandatory talent, a mandatory profession, or similar goal are not supportive, they dictate a life or belief which the child is forced to accept or else be punished. Many children and college age people suffer from anxiety, unhealthy stress, or low self-esteem because they are not measuring up to their family's expectations. I have seen several students have a nervous breakdown because they got a B in two classes for a nursing degree. The expectations of themselves and from others are too focused on perfection with no other options because of the family, education system, or profession. The idea which is prevalent today is that failure is an all consuming fire, especially for those people I just described. Albert Einstein, Thomas Edison, and hundreds of inventories, thinkers, and entrepreneurs have failed over and over in their quest to achievement, but the thing we hear the most is their one or many successes. The difference between these many failures is that failure was not a failure; it was a compass for these men and women who were a success. Try and try again until you succeed is their motto, which is not what the unsupportive family shows to the younger generation.

When we are children, we imitate our parents, friends, people on television, or things in books. We are taught wrong and right from infancy to adulthood, but we pay attention to everything, and that everything can be very damaging if what we see is not right, but wrong or short of the mark. It is no wonder that most people who abuse others, themselves have a history of abuse by someone else in their youth. People are shown many things like fighting, killing, stealing, and many more negative things by close family and friends, and they take this representation as the way life should be. Boxing for instance is a sport; however, if a child is not educated to this fact, then the child will think boxing or fighting is the right thing to do as a life style. It is more influential when the child or teenager sees the same behavior from his/her peers even though the behavior might be unhealthy, illegal, or damaging with long term effects. An example is when there are siblings and extended family; the minor children will more than likely follow the footsteps of the older children or young adults. It is almost like monkey see, monkey do. There is a major problem with this social behavior, because if the older sibling(s) and extended family are behaving or following bad habits, bad behaviors, or bad judgment, the younger children will follow suit and most of the time will exceed the bad behavior, judgment, or habits. What does all this mean? If a big brother smokes cigarettes, does this mean that the younger brother or sister will smoke as well? Not necessarily, because their might be other siblings who don't, the parents night influence the younger child in a more positive way, or the child's friends might discourage the behavior. However, let's put an illegal or damaging substance into the picture.

The make-up of the family and environment for the child will play a major factor in the child following what is right or wrong. The parents are or should be the source of love, wisdom, and authority. The older siblings and friends should also be a source of caring, wisdom, but not authority as we normally see authority of a parent or government. If a child starts to do illegal drugs, the parents and everyone else should be doing whatever they can to stop the behavior and to empower the child to choose wisely so that the behavior is not repeated or attempted. The parents could punish and/or educate the child until they turn blue in the face, and the child may stop, but there is a problem. If for some reason the older sibling, older cousins, or trusted friends are also doing illegal drugs, or abusing legal drugs, then the child is in the middle of a contradiction which has a very strong chance of going wrong. The child sees what wrong looks like in the form of a person the child looks up to, in this case the sibling, cousins, and friends. They are not the authority figures at this point; they are the authority nullifiers I should say, because they directly or indirectly tell the child or teen that what the parents are saying is wrong or not important enough to follow. In fact, even if the child understands that the behavior is illegal, according to the example set by the sibling, cousins, and friends it is okay to do. The child reasons that the drug use can be controlled, is okay to do because the child is not hurting other people, or a few more other reasons that the child, teenager, or young adult will end up using to justify his/her behavior. When things go wrong and the child or teenager comes to a point where hospitalization, detainment or some other consequence occurs, blame will be thrown left and right towards the siblings, friends, and even the parents for not setting the right example or not being forceful enough. The focus should be on getting the child, teenager, or young adult well, and surround him/her with what right looks like. Constant blaming after the fact only sends messages of condemnation, and not healing.

Teaching and setting a right example is what right looks like is all about. We can say that it is a person's own fault for falling into drug abuse, catching a sexually transmitted disease, stealing, or whatever evil lurks in or around our lives. The truth is that we as family and friends have a self appointed responsibility to set a good example. I say it is a responsibility because when we just do whatever we want and set bad examples we are being irresponsible in life. You can go drinking and be responsible by drinking in moderation and not get into trouble, but when you make your behavior open to your younger audience or even teach the younger audience to drink in moderation, you are putting fire in the hands of another person. Everyone is different and you might be willing to accept the consequences of illegal or legal damaging behavior, but you are irresponsible to think that the younger and sometimes older audience can and should also accept or control the consequences you have accepted out of ignorance or research.

Pornography in many homes has been a major problem for children living there. I am talking about the pornography which mom and/or dad might keep in the house for their use and pleasure. The parents might be mature enough to play with pornography and accept the negative consequences, but the child will see it in time even if the material is hidden or locked away. The internet and friends are highways of access to seeing what wrong looks like. The younger generation sees many bad examples, and they follow, because that is what people do as a part of naturally growing up. They follow not because they are weak or naive; they follow blindly because somewhere down the line the people closest to them within the family have not showed them what right looks like. The person has a mind of his/her own, but there is always a level of following in them that is part of leaning. This setting the example is a constant thing, not a once in a while I will do what is right so my child, sibling, or cousin will not stray into the dark side sort of speaking. No, it is a constant loving correction of things around you that you can affect by teaching what right looks like and living what right looks like.

All this sounds like works or things to do, but don't be in

despair. Jesus has done all the work, and all you have to do is look at Him. When you look at Him and see what right looks like, you will do what is right naturally. God in His wisdom has shown you what right looks like in His Son throughout the entire bible. Jesus said in John 15:13, "There is no greater love than this: that a person would lay down his life for the sake of his friends (Bauscher, 2010)." Jesus walked on the Earth and showed us what right looks like and He gave His life for our sake. Jesus is now at the right hand of the Father and still shows us what right looks like through His word and His Holy Spirit. I have talked about common sense reasoning, identity, habits, the spirit, and setting the example. Life is full of joy if you just focus on Jesus and not on all that paint on the wall which we call the world.

Chapter Nine

❧ ----- ❧

What Does Life Have For You

There are many people, who had nothing to show for in respect to money or property, but they are still happy and enjoy their lives. These people might not have money or property, but they might have a wealth of family and friends, and/or can travel around the world with people opening their homes to them. A life of wealth can be material or immaterial. There are times we see a lifestyle full of cars, mansions, a lot of children, many friends, exciting job, and much more, and we imagine how it would be if we could have all of that which the world offers. Even if we have all of that, for some reason there are many people who want more. Then there is the little boy or girl who lives on the street and out of a gift of love someone gives him/her a new pair of shoes, new clothes to wear for the season, and a blanket. That child will see his/her life with eyes of gratitude, not envy or desire for more, or there is a very small possibility that the child we see it as that is how life is. Positive thinking has a place in seeing life or I should say the world for what it is and can be. If you look at the world as an evil place with evil people and very little goodness that touches you, then what does this life or the world have for you, evil? The fact is that this life and this world are not synonymous. The world tells you that material things can fulfill your life, and immaterial things can also fulfill your life. Life itself tells you that the world is a tool, and in order to use it you have to follow its rules and ideals. Rules for the material things, rules like working hard for money, investing wisely, saving for a rainy day, and many more. Ideals like justice for all, fighting for the weak, act honorably to be esteemed, only the fittest survive, don't let yourself get short changed, and many more. What many people don't understand or care to accept is that life as we know it is mixed in with this world and that life is more than having a happy and fulfilling experience.

Life experiences and fate are sometimes blended together by soothsayers/fortune tellers. One day comes along and you fall into hard times. You look for a way out and go job searching, education searching, a fortune teller, money searching, or personal edification searching, but you have so many options. You can grab at get rich quick schemes or fixes, go into illegal options, start an educational or professional development plan, get another or extra job, get depressed, sell possessions you might or might not want, get a loan, ask for charity, or quite a few more. Bon Jovi created a song, "It's my life." It is a testament to what is good in life and how we can chose to live our life while we are full of life and not death. "I'm a Survivor," is another song by Destiny's Child, which depicts the determination of fighting for a good life in the face of adversity. These entertainment channels of what life has to offer are a grain of sand in all the world's beaches, which we accept as part of the world and our life's reflection.

Life is more than just choosing to have a better life, believing in a better life, believing in a better world, or surviving in a world that has fallen. The life which we take for granted is much more than working a job, providing for a family or just yourself, and be merry. There are people who have come to a point where they do not want to live, either due to a mental disorder or they have decided that their life is not worth living. Many just say they want to die in order to get attention so that they can get help, which they really need on many physical, emotional, and spiritual levels. Many people think that living is good if things are going their way, if they have their sex partners, money, luxury items, good looks, power, prestigious job, fame or recognition, and many more things of this world, but if things don't go their way, life is bad. There are also many people who think that living is great no matter what happens because there is life after death and the rewards are far better than the best things we can experience here on Earth. There are those who are in the middle of these two ideas, because they see reality unfold before them when tragedy hits or their belief system is compromised. They believe in an afterlife, but the life which they live in is too real and altering for them. What they have problems with is that life does not always show us in this world what we are told to be eternal blessings, love, and peace. Many people in church are beaten down by not a message of joy, but fire and brimstone or laws which we cannot keep without resting in Jesus.

People are social and emotional in nature, no matter how intellectual or simple minded we might be, we all need to talk to someone and we all show emotions to those we talk to. The interaction causes happiness or conflict. Unfortunately, there seems to be enough conflict that peace is put on the shelf while hatred, war, worry, and fear take control of our lives. The lack of love we see every day with reports of abuse, murders, hate crimes, and many more show us that love may not be eternal or not all it is cracked up to be. Those people who believe in eternal love, peace, and blessings no matter what negative things they see or experience have something which everyone wants to have. People want to know the mysteries in life; they want to be assured that there is life after death or more to life than meets the eye. The people who believe in God's word that Jesus has defeated death and gives us eternal life are the ones with this assurance. In the book of John 11: 25-26 Jesus said, "I am the resurrection and the life; he who believes in Me shall live even if he dies, and everyone who lives and believes in Me shall never die. Do you believe this (NASB, 1990)?"

It is easy for us to comfort someone with a promise for an afterlife. Many 'religions', proclaimed leaders, or groups promise an afterlife, or health and wealth with an afterlife. The catch is that you have to sacrifice your money, your possessions, your time, or your body to receive the health and wealth blessings in this world and in the afterlife. Some people believe that being a good person will result in an afterlife of a reincarnated person who will be a king or someone who holds greater blessings than the last life. If you are a bad person, you will be reincarnated into an inferior animal or a person who will be punished in prison or somewhere terrible. Science would look at this and say, that does not make sense. What happens when a 1,000 mile object in space collides with the Earth and all life to include micro-organisms die? Do we wait a few billion years for life to come about again, only to be engulfed by the Sun when it turns into a Giant Red Star? Or do the lives travel to another planet filled with life in a galaxy far far away to be reincarnated there? Is life a sequence of never ending reincarnations or to an ultimate being that does not need to be reincarnated? The life Christians see is an eternal life where dying in the present physical body is not an end, and the second coming of Jesus will be the beginning of a body which cannot die, be harmed by space, heat, or cold, or anything else and this new body will have your soul in it. There is no reincarnation into a temporary alien body until the next reincarnation. There is a promise for the afterlife, but there is also health and wealth in our present life. Yes, there is health and wealth, but do not be troubled because you don't have to spend money or sign a contract of blood with anyone. All you have to do is listen and believe to what is said about Jesus.

Life is a constant experience which we all want to keep; we all have an urge to live in our deepest nightmare when we face death. We yearn to feel happy when someone shows us love, gives us pleasure, or listens to you. We yearn to see good things happen to us and others. We yearn to have hope that evil will be destroyed and good will prevail. But even though life does have many good things to offer us in this present world, we let the world steer us into believing that joy, justice, and righteousness is not met if life does not go our way. Life in this world in other words, is not fair because this life is not meeting my needs or desires. Life in Jesus is beyond this world and focusing on Him will give all of what we need or desire in life or this world.

Chapter Ten

❧ ----- ☙

Is Life Fair or Not Fair

Many people have this idea that life is unfair. They blame God, their parents, or other people for their misfortune or miserable life situation. There are religious advertisers in the world that say the world is full of sin and bad things fall on both the good and bad people. Sin is so ever present that God could not exist or be a God of love. Children learn this concept of fairness at an early age when they see hypocritical actions, or mixed messages of parents or people who have the power to give and take away. You see two criminals go to court with the same offense, similar factors and are both found guilty, but one is given three years while the other is given the death penalty, because one plea bargained and the other did not. Was life fair? The criminal that gets out in two years goes and kills a person, then gets life with probation in 15 years. The other person on the other hand is executed and DNA evidence proves that the person was innocent after all. Was life fair? Now, there is a child who tries her hardest to help out mom at home, and the teachers at school. She loves her parents and out of nowhere a family friend kidnaps her and brutally kills her. Is that fair? In another part of the country a man goes on a killing spree and ends up retiring at an old age, he lies to his wife everyday by pretending he is a good man, but instead he goes off every now and then to kill a prostitute or simply cheat on his wife. He ends up having children who think he is the best thing since slice bread, and the history books in a diary or eulogy speaks of this good man who never stepped into a jail cell. Is that fair? If Jesus being sinless and innocent was it fair that he died for your sins, even though he willingly took your place. No, it is not fair, and we accept this fact, but not when things happen to us that are unfair.

Understandably, injustice is classified as unfair and when justice is done, then it is fair. There is a problem with this logical view. If a person does not believe in God or a supreme being that has a final say in his/her future, then this view is absolutely correct according to the belief of that person and maybe according to what they consider as the truth. Now if a person believes in God or a supreme being, then this view is not measured by just or unjust, fair or unfair; it is measured in accordance with what God says is fair or unfair, and that justice is His. Some people think that if justice is not met here on Earth, that in heaven it will be forgiven or something. Many people think that God is judging everyone now on Earth, and when they die, they will be punished in hell or rewarded in heaven. There are also people who think that God will judge everyone on judgment day and then people will go to the respective locations of heaven or hell. No matter which way you look at it God is the judge and punisher. What many people accept is that God has the power to enforce His judgments and that they are based on God's laws. However, many people don't want to accept this until they are face to face with death or God Himself shows up in front of them with brimstone and lighting, or something like that before they give in and acknowledge God's truth and authority. In the meantime they pursue their own pleasures or beliefs that say otherwise.

Another aspect about justice is that people don't accept things concerning God's justice because they think that there must be swift and perfect justice in the face of evil and what people think is true justice. There are millions of court proceedings every year that make the news which are classified as high profile cases in that local district, across state boundaries, or across country boundaries. There are daily shows on several different channels on forensics or investigations talking about murder, rape, fraud, theft, and a few more that show the public the side of justice or injustice which is in their neighborhood.

One case, which is recent and with great controversy, is the State of Florida vs. Casey Marie Anthony for the murder of Caylee Anthony in 2008. The trial was in 2011, and the evidence given by both the prosecutor and defense was enough to cover several weeks of trial. The verdict was not guilty to first and second degree murder, which is what the great controversy is focused on. In the end, the exact reason for Caylee's death is still a mystery except to Casey and God. As a mother, she had a responsibility and was the last one to have seen Caylee. Accident or no accident, Casey will have to answer for her action or inaction to God. Many people feel justice was not met, because humankind has this idea that if they do not administer their own justice, then justice is not being met. Casey is in hiding and will probably have to live the rest of her life that way because there are people who are willing to go to jail or be put to death just as long as Casey is killed (punished) for her alleged murder of her daughter. I am not here to take sides, I personally think Casey should had been punished for neglect, lying, and tampering with an investigation at the very least, of which she was only punished for tampering and lying. Two years timed served while waiting for the trial, is that justice? In this fallen world, it is justice and God will make all things come together for our good. Because of the verdict and controversy Caylee Anthony's Law was passed and requires parents to report missing children. Parents like Casey with a similar situation will not get such a mild sentence now that the law is enacted.

In accordance to the laws of God in the Old Testament, there is an age of accountability. If a child is not of age and dies, that child will not go to hell, but God will take the child to be with Him in Heaven. It is a great tragedy for this world that Caylee died at an early age, and shame on those who think it was an act of God. Caylee died because a person or people on Earth did not watch out for her, or she was intentionally killed. But justice is partially served, because Caylee's spirit is now in heaven with Jesus. If Casey has not accepted Jesus as her savior, she will not be in heaven. In the meantime Casey is in a prison where she will have to look over her shoulder for as long as she lives only to end up in eternal damnation, barring she accepts God's grace. Justice is not blind to God, but to this world it can be twisted. God will not allow the twisting to dominate His justice, so don't worry too much if things do not go the way you think they should.

This brings up a point that should be noted. The fall of man also caused the world to suffer judgment. When Adam and Eve ate of the tree of knowledge of good and evil, they understood what sin was, sinned, and gave their power over death to Satan. God gave the law to man after He took His select people, the Hebrews, out of Egypt. The law which God gave man was to show man that he was not able to keep the law and therefore not be able to get the authority over death back from Satan. When Jesus fulfilled the law by not breaking any of the laws, and gave us victory, Jesus gave us the power over death through Him. However, the Earth is still waiting to be cleansed of the evil which has infected it. You might ask, well if Jesus took sin away, then why is the Earth still affected by sin and why are we still here? Sin is not the factor in why we are still here. If I were to tell you that God gave you a free will and that you had the power to decide to follow God or not, then you might say okay, well what else can I say – yes or no? Now what if I told you God just gave Jesus the keys to heaven for all those who want to enter. Are you going to ask God, your next door neighbor, the locks smith, or Jesus to use the keys so you can enter heaven? Common sense would suggest that you ask Jesus, the man with the keys. Now imagine that you are the first one He told this good news to and you tell Him that you want to follow Him and to let you into heaven. Now, Jesus grants your wish because you have accepted that Jesus has the power to get you to heaven. While you are alive on Earth, you follow Jesus because you said you would and Jesus is going to make sure you are empowered with His blessings to be able to follow Him. Now the second person does not accept the truth that Jesus has the keys to heaven; the third as well, the fourth person accepts Him, and so on. If Jesus wants everyone to get the opportunity to know and ask Him to let them into heaven, then Jesus would have to wait for everyone to hear and answer Him. Jesus loves everyone and wants them to accept what God has done for them, but not everyone will say yes to Jesus. There will be a time when the offer stops and Jesus has to let all the Earth become like heaven, without sin.

The second coming of Jesus is the end of the offer, and the beginning of a new Earth and new Heaven. Yes, life is not fair in this world, because it is infected with evil. There is a measure of justice in the world due to enforcement of the law, people, and God; but in the end justice will be God's, everyone has their fair chance in the form of free will, and everyone will get their fair reward or punishment. On a practical sense, life is unfair if you see it that way. The fact that we are in a fallen world says that life is fair because you still live. You may not have a billion dollars, but you a living body. You might be crippled, but you are alive and there are people around you that love you. You might be in jail for something you did not do, but you are alive and can be a witness for someone so they do not go to a prison that will never have parole but eternal anguish. People might be abused daily, but there is hope here and now, and their reward will be great in heaven and the new Earth. The focus of what we think is important is also what shapes our idea of fairness and justice, but knowing that justice will be met can comfort us in times of temporary anguish. God is faithful and just to punish injustice. In light of all this, we as good people made righteous by the blood of Jesus must act in the face of evil. Life might not be fair in this world, but we must try to make it fair for everyone.

Chapter Eleven

ॐ ----- ॐ

The Truth

Truth is defined as the actual state of a matter, conformity with fact or reality; a verified or indisputable fact, proposition, principle, or the like (Dictionary.com, 2012). There is a saying, "Liar, liar pants on fire." Everyone seems to know what a lie is, but do we know what the truth is? I use the word seems, because to some degree the truth can be subjective because the observer can be mistaken, flawed, or ignorant. Likewise the source can be flawed or inconsistent. There is a man and a woman sitting outside on a blanket staring out into the setting sun. The clouds in the sky are lit by a red aura which is simply the air particles absorbing or reflecting the normally white and yellow light on a noon day, changing the light spectrum that is observed to red. The woman says how pretty the red sky and clouds are, but the man says that they are yellow. Now, what is the truth and who is speaking the truth? It would help if I added another piece of information and that is the man has deuteranopia. So the truth is that the clouds and sky around it are giving off a red spectrum of light. The woman is right saying that the clouds are red. The man on the other hand is wrong in the sense of reality, but he is speaking the truth that the clouds are yellow, because that is the color spectrum he sees due to his red-green color blindness. In fact to him yellows, whites, and blues dominate his life with reds and greens being something he might not have ever experienced. However, the man is speaking the truth from his perspective, and is not lying because the clouds are really red. Does this sound like a logical and true way of seeing things? Is it logical to say the truth is that the color of the sky is red, because the woman is not color blind and about 90% of the population is not color blind? If not, then what is the truth? Okay, now that the man and woman finish saying what they see, another man approaches them and he has a pair of goggles which see into the ultraviolet spectrum of both the visible and invisible to the human eye. The goggles translate data it sees to a representation of what actually is being received by the goggles. The goggles show you a spectrum of purple, but of course the color blind man does not see the purple the woman and second man see through the goggles. In addition the goggles reveal that the sky is purple, not red. So now, there are three different interpretations of a color of a light spectrum which does not change except on the receiver or observer side. The truth is that what people see is a color and it differs due to biological or goggle circumstances.

The truth of the source is more or less established by its existing or being. If a label is given to an object, like a table, then that object will be perceived to be consistent to that label across the board if it is taught that way. If you are taught that a shoe is a table, then when a person shows you a table and tells you that it is a table; you will think that it is a shoe and what that person is saying is not true. So, my point is that there has to be a consensus to how things and ideas are labeled/called/named, or there will be confusion between truth and false. Note that I did not say there has to be a consensus as to what is true or falsehood. What is true will always be true as long as the situation does not change. If a boy, named Robert, is physically a baby at an age of one, it is true that Robert is a baby; but when he grows to be a teen, a young man, a middle aged man, and then an elderly man, the truth is that he changed and is no longer a baby, but something else.

We tend to look at truth in a scientific way, and so we should since we are in a world where there are laws and science that can explain things. But, what about those things which we cannot see or confirm because they are beyond our ability to really know as truth. An example of this is history. We are very sure that as long as a person does not lie or does not perceive things incorrectly we can talk to a person who is a witness to an event and accept it as fact limited to the memory of the person. If a book is written and the information is collaborated with other sources, whether experimental, oral, physical, or even information within the document itself, we can more or less accept it as a truth. However, if I decide to tell a story about a family or myself which is completely made up, but declare that is it a factual story or event, then is the historical event the truth? This happened many times in history where the victors wrote what they wanted to be their version of the truth in history. Not all victors wrote their version of the truth, which is why it is important to verify what is thought to be true with other sources when it comes to history.

The other aspect is not completely time related, but spatial or metaphysical in nature. There is a saying that goes something like this, "If a tree falls in the forest and there is no one around to hear it fall, did it make a sound?" I would comment on this saying by asking, "Did the tree even fall?" Yes – No; how do you know unless you were there to hear it or go see that it fell. Do you accept that it did make a sound because you have heard other trees when they fell? There is a lot of psychological and philosophical thought involved which questions reality, but from a practical sense of logic, science, and even spiritual reality the tree did make a sound, history is captive to the writer at the time, and we can understand that there are limitations in knowing the truth or falsehood.

The truth is more than something that is correct, or as the definition put it; an indisputable fact. Jesus said in the book of John 14:6, ""I am the way and the truth and the life. No one comes to the Father except through me (NASB, 1990)." In John 1:17, John writes, "For the Law was given through Moses; grace and truth were realized through Jesus Christ (NASB, 1990)." Jesus is attributed to be truth and grace, and He himself claims to be the truth. I have heard many people say that Jesus was a great prophet of God. The problem with this saying is that if Jesus were a great prophet, then he was a great false prophet. A prophet of God speaks for God and always speaks the truth. Not once did a true prophet ever say he was the Christ, God, or the Son of God. Jesus did claim to be the Son of God and God Himself, as I AM in John 8:58, "Jesus said to them, 'Truly, truly, I say to you, before Abraham was born, I AM.'" Jesus either is the Son of God, God in the flesh, or He is a liar and not the truth. You can either accept the truth in everything that is said of Jesus, or you can attack the truthfulness of the bible. There is a book called, Jesus Interrupted, and the author like many others claim that the bible came about in a corrupted fashion, and the influence of humans with the original authors, and translations make the bible a contradiction on itself. The author is completely biased and prejudice of the bible and completely takes things out of context. He is a scholar of the New Testament; however, his research is bias, which places his conclusions into great pitfalls. The author is also a believer that God does not exist because there is so much sin in the world; hence the God of the Bible could not possibly exist or be God for allowing sin to go supposedly ramped; which is not a surprise as to his claims which are not logical, objective or researched properly. It might sound like I hate this guy, but I don't, I simply disagree with things which he says, for example. He states that Jesus was a follower of John the Baptist's teachings. In reading the New Testament, nowhere did John the Baptist declare himself to be the Christ or God. John the Baptist was the herald of the King, which is Jesus. Never has any king come on the scene only to follow the herald around or his teachings, which was repent and behold the Lamb, our Savior.

If you had super powers which include the ability to create planets, stars, and galaxies, do you think that you can make sure that humans do not put whatever blots of ink they want in a book which you want people to read. Many other books or documents tried to get inside the bible, but as God would have it the Christian Bible has 66 books which make-up the Bible. There are additional books in a handful of other denominations like the Catholic Church and Eastern Orthodox Old Testament. Regardless, there is a finite number of a consistent collection of books or writings within one book written by multiple authors and the one inspiring Holy Spirit of God, which we can compare and have bible interpret bible. In 'Jesus Interrupted', the author says that the bible contradicts itself, but in reality the books do not contradict themselves and all point towards Jesus, in His person, in types and shadows, or self witness by God and Jesus Himself. Jesus who is the truth; not just another character in a book or books to proclaim a religion or tell a history of God and man. The truth is constant as Jesus is constant and eternal.

Chapter Twelve

౽ ----- ౼

What Is Grace

G race has several meanings and includes elegance and beauty; however, the grace I am talking about is the unmerited and undeserved favor of God towards you and me. But what does that mean really, what is the unmerited and undeserved favor of God? All you have to do is look at Jesus to understand what was meant in John 1:17, "grace and truth were realized through Jesus Christ (NASB, 1990)." The general Christian teaching is that grace is unmerited mercy that God gave to us by sending His Son to die on the cross to give us eternal salvation. I do not fully agree with this because as we look at the person of Jesus we can see that grace is not mercy or salvation alone, but righteousness and love. I want to point out that mercy and love are not the same things, and salvation for us involves judgment and righteousness. People for some reason have this idea that Jesus took our place on the cross because God had mercy on us and forgave you and me for our sins and that is why we are not going to be judged and go to hell. Mercy is what has kept God from punishing us immediately after we sinned. Mercy is God's patience almost like a father or mother having patience with an unruly teenager. Mercy is like a governor commuting a person's death sentence, but you must understand that punishment will be demanded now or later by God.

Biblically speaking, the bible tells us that Jesus came down to Earth to save us because God the father and the Son loved us even though we were still sinners, and when Jesus took our place on the cross, Jesus was judged and punished by God the Father for all eternity. Jesus, who did not deserve to be judged and punished at all, took our place because of love, not mercy. The person who has honestly accepted Christ Jesus as their Savior has already being judged and punished in Jesus on the cross, that is why a believer will go to heaven and not hell. Believers do not wait for Jesus to come back so we can be judged to find out if we will go to hell or heaven; we wait to see His full victory when all evil will be thrown into the lake of eternal fire, and the new heaven and Earth will be made for us to live in with perfect peace, no sin, never aging, and forever one with God. This is why it is said that the grace of God is a gift, not as a reward or prize; because we did nothing to deserve it nor did we accomplish anything to merit it. Jesus is grace, Jesus is God's gift to us, Jesus is the one who stepped in front of certain punishment and death for us so we could live with God himself; where He is; and not have sin be our essence, but the righteousness of Jesus be our essence. God has to judge and punish sin, because the essence of sin is completely contrary to God.

If you are king, a chieftain, a leader of your home, a person of authority in your mansion, and you create ten people who you raise from birth. You teach them all you know about everything good, but there is a problem. One of the ten listens to your butler who lies to him and teaches him about bad things. That person infects the rest of the ten, and out of the ten only two continue to follow you, but they still struggle in doing what is good. You tell all ten to leave the house, because if they stayed in your presence, you would have to punish them immediately because of the law. All ten leave your house, but you own all the land, air, and sea. In addition, your kingdom is run by your laws and your will. What happens next is that your butler has become a leader of sorts and leaves the house every now and then only to lead a band of your ten people to do bad and fight against you. You love the ten so much that you tell your only biological son to go gather the ten and bring them home. Your son goes out into your kingdom and finds your ten, but only two listen to him, and the other eight want to kill your son because he has promised them a good life with you but they want to live their evil lives on their terms, so they think that by killing your son they don't need to answer to you. You have to uphold your laws, due to justice simply because without your laws being met, then chaos will reign and not you. In the end your son knows that you will punish the evil which has befallen your house and the kingdom. So your son goes to you and takes all the punishment for the injustice they ten have committed. The son promised the two and any other who might decide to accept your offer to return home that they would be allowed back into the house with him. You have already punished you son for the sake of the ten. You will bring your son back to life and let him punish the ones who did not accept your offer to return. The ones who did not accept your son will be punished because justice must be met and if they do not want the son to pay for them, then they must pay, and be punished until death along with the butler who betrayed you. This story is simplistic and similar to the parable Jesus said in Mark 12:1-12. There is truth in both, a righteous judge must judge righteously, there cannot be any compromise. Grace is the full extent of righteousness by God judging and punishing all of our sins, past, present and future in the body of Jesus. The judgment of God in the second coming is His wrath which is the full extent of righteousness on those who rejected His Son and desired after their own evil ways. Jesus has redeemed you from the judgment of God, but Jesus cannot redeem you if you reject His gift of grace unto salvation.

Imagine if I give you a life saver and put it in your hands while you are treading water or more likely drowning in the ocean. There is attached to the life saver a rope that goes to a ship, but you reject it and swim away, knowing that the ship cannot stop or turn around; you can call or describe this ship as time. I keep trying to help you and swim next to you so you don't have to worry about letting go due to fatigue, and you reject my help and swim away from me for whatever reason, maybe you see or hear someone else saying they can help you, but they are going away from the ship and are lying to you. Maybe you want to look at the colorful fish in the water, but the thing is you reject me and want someone else to save you or think you can save yourself. There will be a point when once the ship gets to its destination that those who allowed me to help them will be on dry land and alive while the others who rejected me will be dead at the bottom of the ocean or in a shark's stomach.

I have children, and there are times when I have to let them make mistakes. Granted, they grow and learn from their mistakes, but like I told them during their teen and young adult years, "I am not going to let you drown in a lake of mistakes before I decide to step in to pull you out and resuscitate you back to life." There is usually an intervention involved when drugs, alcohol, sex, gangs, or things like that become a red flag in my watchful eyes of the people I love and care about. If the intervention works; great, but in the end a decision by a person who has free will is responsible for their decisions. This is one reason people who get to an age of 18 in the US are legally held liable for committing illegal acts based on their wrong decisions. Jesus came to us at the right time and has given us room to accept Him before we make too many mistakes and are completely lost in our lives without Him. For the believer, the grace we have inside of us is Jesus in the form of the Holy Spirit. Our spirit along with His spirit empowers us to live in a world full of sin, but still be righteous and full of God's favor. For the non-believer or religious, you know if Jesus is your Savior in your heart, and if you don't then you have not accepted this gift of salvation, and you are living by the mercy of God which does have an expiration date.

Chapter Thirteen

• ----- •

This World and That Which Lasts Forever

Science fiction stories, books, shows, and movies have been around for about a century. Star Trek, Dr. Who, Babylon 5, Star Wars, and many more sci-fi fans know that without science fiction in our lives, a man landing on the moon might still be an unrealized accomplishment in the world. A history of generations of family professions, beliefs, culture, traditions, languages, accomplishments, defeats, and much more are a part of us and this world we live in. The world tells us that if we fight in the face of courage or have victory over an epic enemy, that we will be remembered for an eternity. We hear and see this in the movie Gladiator when Russell Crowe's character, General Maximus Decimus Meridius, says, "What we do in life, echoes in eternity." In a way he is right, but not in the context which he was using it or the context which many people view it. The worldly context is to have a virtue or destiny which people will honor and praise, but what happens when a person performs an action that is completely the opposite of the virtues which

Maximus was talking about? There are many people in history which have not been forgotten, and until the new Earth and Heaven comes, their legacy will be echoed in this world, but not eternity. What is sad is that some, not all, of these people are idolized by other people. These people which made the top 50 most evil people include : Ivan the Terrible, Adolf Hitler, Attila The Hun, Caligula, Idi Amin, Nero, Pol Pot, Vlad the Impaler, Torquemada, Rasputin, Jack the Ripper, Francisco Pizarro, Joseph Stalin, Elizabeth Bathory, Katherine Knight, Irma Grese, Ilse Koch, Mary Ann Cotton, Jiang Qing, Oliver Cromwell, Shirō Ishii, Ted Bundy, Javed Iqbal, John Haigh, Gilles de Rais, Richard Trenton Chase, Jeffrey Dahmer, Albert Fish, and tragically the list continues way beyond the hundred thousand. The actions we do or don't do will give us a name in this world, but so what? Do we do things to put our name in the history books, or do we do things because it is the right thing to do, without any intention of getting recognition or praise from other people? Do we do things which matter in our lives, or do we do things that matter only to the world?

A man and woman marry with great dreams and hopes for their future. They were able to travel the world, help out many people through charities, help raise theirs and other's peoples' children, but for some reason in the face of the great depression, they commit suicide and take their three children with them to the grave. This type of situation is not an isolated event in life and has occurred worldwide from ancient history until recently. The world says that it is okay to give up if you lose your livelihood, save face (avoid embracement) by killing yourself, or dying is a virtue if you believe in a religion that says killing yourself or death is required. The people who are praised and cherished by family and friends, who put their effort into what lasts, and who see life in this world as a temporary layover before getting to heaven, tend to focus on what matters in their life, not what the world says should matter to you.

A million things pop out of the world to entice all of our senses, and then our mind and body. There are many wonderful things we have or can experience in our lives. The soft touch of a silk blanket, smell of a sweet scent, taste of a marvelous fruit, the vision of white clouds soaring past a mountain peak, or the sound of soothing chimes due to an ocean breeze. On the other side of the field there is grass but not greener; instead it is black where there are terrible things which we do or can experience. The pain of a bone disease, the smell of rotting flesh, the taste of rotting fruit, or the vision of your loved one being tortured in front of you. What does all this have to do with the world, or for that matter, it sounds more like our lives, not the world. Remember that I said this world we live in is a fallen world? Before Adam and Eve sinned and fell from grace (God's favor), the whole Earth was a perfect paradise. There were no thorns, nothing was rotting, no weather problems, no pollution, no animals eating other animals, no diseases, no allergies, no death, no lack of food, or anything evil or bad as we can only imagine. When Adam sinned, he gave his authority over the Earth and himself to Satan. When Jesus rose from the dead, He took back all authority from Satan. The plan is set and once Jesus comes back, He will have a major house cleaning which many people fear and know as judgment day. The whole Earth was cursed due to Adam's fall, so when Adam fell, so did the world. Now what we have is paradise infected with the opposite of paradise, I call this mixture as being plain and absolutely 'messed up'. This world still does have glimpses of paradise when we can feel a nice cool sun set at a beach with fresh salty air going through your nostrils. A soft hug from the person you love, and a gentle massage of your back tells you that this life in this world can be wonderful. It is wonderful, but it is also flawed and should not be your sole reason for living. At the same time, there is a person out there who is suffering from malnourishment, heat stroke, an animal attack, a deadly poison, or a very bad day at work. There are many people who see themselves with a flexible life and believe that things can be good or bad, and should be what we make it. This attitude is usually for the person who wants something to conquer, an excuse to misbehave, or an excuse to feel accepted and not condemned for being in a fallen state. Real paradise does not have this flexibility of having a possibility of turning into a hell; however, since our lives are mixed in with this world/wall, the best thing we can hope for is to focus only on the paradise side.

Jumping out of a perfectly good airplane has wonderful sensations which thrill seekers cherish deep in their memories. I was one of those plane jumpers, and even when things don't go so good and your landing becomes an ugly fight with the ground, tree trunk, ledge of a cliff, a big rock, or another person, the memories can still remain cherished or turn into fear which turns into avoidance. For a non-thrill seeker, the experience can be a revelation to something fun, or a nightmare which keeps you deep inside a plane. Going on many amusement park rides can be fun, but there are dangers which this world brings as part of a fallen world. Now imagine that you are in heaven, and they have a 100 mile long roller coaster that lasts 10 minutes, where you are upside down, backwards, sideways, and forwards, with no danger, no shaking seats that make you bang your ears on the body rails, no whiplash, no one vomiting on you; just a perfect fun and exhilarating ride. The world has perfect times, but this is not perfect paradise or a perfect world because those times do not last forever.

Many wealthy people have spent a large portion of their adult time amassing money and property, and a few of them end up killing a spouse, cheat on their spouse, get involved with an addiction, or turn against people with a scourge mentality because they don't have a fulfilling life. A fulfilling life that fills your soul with satisfaction if not complete joy because you have a family who loves and cares about you, employees that turn to you because they truly respect and want to work for you, or a boss who praises you as a person, and many more reasons to be fulfilled. However, the fullness you might feel is not because you accomplished something, your emotions were given their reward, or you found a better way of thinking. The fullness you have is from the things which last forever. The world can satisfy you for a moment, this is easily seen when you eat your favorite food like the best turkey dinner, steak and eggs, ice cream Sunday, or a lobster dinner. You can scarf down a box of your favorite cookies, but no matter how great it tastes or full you get, you will be hungry again before the day ends. You can be happy one day when you make employee of the year, and get a pay raise; but in ten years the satisfaction of your accomplishment can be shrugged off with a casual nod as you have become the general manager, owner of the company, or homeless. The richest man in the world and the poorest man in the world, monetarily speaking, will both die and none of their earthly possessions will hitch a ride with their spirits.

The things of the world do not last forever which include a legacy in human history, self fulfillment, or self enjoyment. I say self, because there are things that last forever and anything that is self involved does not. The Apostle John mentions love as one thing which will last forever. The bible teaches us that God is love, and since God is eternal, so is love. The love you have which comes from God is eternal. Your spirit will last forever too. Whether it will be forever in hell or in the new Earth and heaven, is up to you. The fact that the world we live in is a fallen world does not mean we fall with it, in fact what it means is that the people in the world and the world itself needs us to witness to them the eternal salvation we have in Jesus and also to love each other now not until we get to heaven. On other personal aspects in this world, a child's laughter on his/her fourth birthday is priceless, and eternal. A big hug for your loved ones, to a good friend, or even to someone in need of a hug is also eternal. A good deed done with an honest heart and with love will not go unnoticed by God. Accepting Jesus and worshipping Him will not go unnoticed. Loving your wife, or following your husband as Jesus loved the church and as Jesus gave himself to the church, will not go unnoticed by God. We have talked about thinking or wisdom, habits, what defines you, Jesus as truth and grace, what mercy is, the spirit in you, and a world that does not last, but you will last and your decisions and actions will determine if you chose correctly. I am not claiming that this world is doomed so you just need to accept any tragedy, evil, or bad thing that comes your way. No. there is a plan and in that plan God has given you victory. God has given you victory because Jesus was, still is, and will always be victorious.

Many people hate health and wealth preachers; however, there is a difference between what the world calls health and wealth and what God calls His favor. When you see a preacher tell you that God wants you to prosper and if you use your faith by giving money then the blessing will come, that should bring up a red flag. God never required Abraham, noted for being the father of faith, to give money in order to be blessed. Abraham was blessed and was rich, with livestock, silver, and gold. Abraham gave ten percent of his wealth to God which God gave him, after he was blessed. Abraham did not use his faith by sacrificing something, but by recognizing that God was his reason for being and staying wealthy. Abraham lived to be well into 175 years, and he did not have any pains or illness according to biblical accounts. In fact, Sarah, Abraham's wife, was 90 years old when a king wanted her for his wife because she was more beautiful than the 20 year old women in the entire kingdom. Sarah also gave birth to her first son at age 91, and lived to be about 120 year old. Abraham was so blessed that everyone around him prospered. Not once did God require Abraham to give something he had in order to be blessed or loved. Grace preachers today say, you can reign in life, not because you give to the church or sacrifice something you have, but because Jesus has all the blessings poured out in front of you, all you got to do is look to Jesus and receive from Him. When you are Jesus conscious and believe, you are using faith. Faith is believing that God can supply and then receiving. Jesus on many occasions said to His disciples, "Oh you of little faith." He didn't say oh you of little prayer, little fasting, little giving, little following. No, He meant oh you of little trusting and taking from Me. There is no limit to what Jesus can supply, so why do you doubt – that is the lack of faith which Jesus speaks of. Apart from the blessings we see and acknowledge as coming from God, we do get blessed when we least expect it. People like to use the word lucky. No, you are not lucky, you are blessed, a blessing which rains on everyone. Before I became a Christian, I was for the most part a very smart, very healthy, very humble, and average looking young man, who had started college at age 16, went into the military at 17, made the rank of Sergeant at 18, and was the best thing since sliced bread. The worst thing was there was no human at that time around me that could tell me otherwise. Until God came into my life and He really did humble me. I looked back into my life, and saw that if it wasn't for an act of God's intervention I would have died from a gunshot at the age of 4 when my brother and I found a gun in the house. The gun did go off, but not until it was pointed away from my head. The Being 737 airplane which I flew in to Egypt in 1985 decided to crash a week later. The places we moved to had the best environments for my education and social life. The leaders and mentors in my life were instrumental in defining my character which now is focused on God. The lifelong friends that I made since I was 15 year old kept me away from drugs and other illegal activities. Keep in mind that I was not surrounded by Christian people, almost all of the people around me was from what is called a secular world. So what does this world have to offer, and what really matters to you that will last forever? That is up for you to decide, if you want to get temporary satisfaction coming from this world, or focus on the things which will give you lasting satisfaction coming from Jesus.

Chapter Fourteen

ॐ ----- ॐ

What Do You Live For

N ow that you know there is hope in this world to be happy, experience good things, and to let Jesus take care of you; you can live without fear, condemnation, enslavement, or addictions. You get to live to see the next day, and God's blessings for that day. Now, wait a minute, you have no idea of what I am living through as a nightmare night and day. I agree; you could be having the worst day or year of your life right now. You can continue to look at your life as hell, but you can also start now to live for something, or not live for nothing, which is more or less hell. Life is full of love and energy. If you have problems getting motivated or are around the wrong crowd, then try your best to be exposed to and stay exposed to positive influences. Stop looking at things which are negative in nature, like the news, comedies which make fun of people – especially with vulgarity, shows about evil spirits, ghosts, demons, murder, sexual promiscuity, or reality shows which show outrageous or disrespectful behavior. I am not saying be ignorant by not watching the news, but limit and censor your viewing or reading of things in the media.

The best thing you could possible do is ask God to come into your life, or if you are already a believer, is focus on Jesus, by reading or learning about Him every day. When you look into the bible, look for a revelation of Jesus and rest in Him every day, not just in your time of need. If you are not one to accept Jesus just yet, the other thing you could do is look at yourself and ask yourself, where do you see yourself in a year from now or a month from now. How did you get to where you are now? It only matters that you know how you got there, but whatever you do, do not take it personal. Do not blame yourself; focus on the mechanics of how you got there. What was done is done, blaming yourself will not help. However, taking action to change your situation and actions to prevent the situation from happening again is what will help you.

An example of this is if you ignore your parents, teachers, and other information sources and you make some really careless decisions only to incur $80,000 credit card debt, not to mention a house and car debt. Your spending habits and lack of money management skills have contributed to this. Your quest to get rich quick has also contributed to your failed business endeavors. Your loved ones also going crazy with bad spending habits do not help the situation. You take a step back, and use some common sense reasoning. You stop blaming and start changing. You know that you must want to change in order to change your current situation. So, you cut the cards, make a budget, do as much research as possible for reducing debt, contact your creditors and see what can be done. You hopefully pray about it and trust that God will help you. You budget a saving plan for a rainy day, the rest of the money should be focused on living essentials, and the rest on reducing debt. Recreational things should be reduced or eliminated. You should be seeking a better or steady job, so your budget can work properly. You make a menu so you can budget your food expenditure better. You stop addictions or bad habits which cost you money, like smoking, drinking coffee, drinking sodas, eating out, wasting food, wasting electricity, and the like. You need to get someone to help you out, so you need to have a support system. The support system can be a book(s), videos, a reliable person, or the internet. Debt collectors will be after you and you have to stay focused and know how to accept their help or bypass them. You have to be patient and understand that there will be problems on the road to recovery, whether it is debt, drugs, homelessness, abuse, alcoholism, education or work related. If you are persistent and determined, you will in time get out of your problem.

I have talked about problems in life. Life does not guarantee that you will feel happiness, or get what you need or want. Life is an experience which can be sour and desiring like Taz Sour Pops, or Lemonheads. Seek out the good things in life, appreciate the good things in life, fix the things you can fix, and let God/Jesus fix the things you can't fix. Life has many things for you. I have seen many people whose lives were filled with death, drugs, abuse, and demonic influences, but they are now witnesses of God's salvation and blessing for anyone who wants to hear and accept salvation and blessings. The people who are living a upper and middle class lifestyle, go to church, but seem like they are not getting anywhere are the ones who are most vulnerable. They are vulnerable to the status quo; to the world at large. They are the people who have problems behind doors, not because they are stagnating, but because they are not trying to find peace in their lives. When you are looking constantly to Jesus, you cannot but help to step into a life full of energy and fulfillment.

Do not listen to those people who tell you that life is about seeking Jesus and being like Jesus, and so you must keep God's commandments with Jesus' help. Do not listen to those people who tell you that you must do this, or do that, and if you don't you cannot enter the kingdom of God. Jesus said in John 14:6, ""I am the way and the truth and the life. No one comes to the Father except through me (NASB, 1990)." Jesus said in John 6:47-48, "Truly, truly, I say to you, he who believes has eternal life. I am the bread of life (NASB, 1990)." Jesus has given you a better way; He has fulfilled the law so you wouldn't have to follow, give, and serve on your own power. If you focus on Jesus, His love, righteousness, salvation, wisdom, power, health, prosperity, hope, discipline, and His love will empower you to step into God's will. You follow, give and serve because you are righteous, because you want to out of your heart which is one with the heart of Jesus. Jesus said He is the life. Jesus gives you true life, and common sense would say that if Jesus is the life, then what we live for should be for Jesus, not this world or ourselves.

The supply of God is not just eternal for the materialistic, but immaterial as well, which includes your soul and spirit. Peace is one of the immaterial that Jesus gives to us to a degree which the world cannot give. The peace of Jesus can change everything in your material world and all things will be subject to your degree of peace. When you let Jesus be your peace, you can go into a room and your peace will be contagious. It is your peace because Jesus has specifically given you His peace. A peace that has patience, is understanding, is full of God's love, and trusts that God is in control. Life, love, peace, hope, and power comes to you in Jesus as a gift which is enough reason to live for in this world that others may also live a life more abundantly.

Many people are in despair thinking that this world is going downhill into the pit of hell. They are wrong because it is going uphill, and it is not going into limbo or hell. It is going into God's presence where everything will be made right. We will stand in front of God in His throne room and life will have a real meaning to us that will be horrifying or the most wonderful time of our lives. Terrifying if we have rejected His Son, and are sentenced to eternal hell fire; or we will be praised for being a good and faithful child of God. The life we have waiting for us in heaven and the new Earth, can be had now in this fallen world. The lie which many people have believed is that we cannot have prosperity or health because we are not following God's will, but in fact we are only fighting the reality that we are blessed, are an adopted son/daughter of God, and all things work for our good by the power which Jesus has in Heaven and on Earth. There is no defeat for the believer, even in death. If a believer dies, he or she will go to be with Jesus in Heaven, where we will have perfect peace and can walk with Jesus in His perfect garden. Life is not good for the person who is not saved, who has not accepted Jesus, because when that person dies, he/she will not be with Jesus.

Now aside from dying, the good things we enjoy in life are ours to embrace, but are not ours to worship. We use the word love too much and attribute it to the world and sometimes life. People say things all the time like: I love to fight, I love my life, I love talking on my cell, I love to drink, I love to play poker, or I love to eat. Many people use the word love as a strong description, which is grammatically correct, but some people use the word so much that they lose the meaning or intent behind it. The idea can also turn in the opposite direction where they have a very strong attraction to a person or celebrity. They end up worshiping the person or an idea and then the word love once again loses its intent or meaning. The love we have in life should be more than an intense feeling of compassion; it is a caring attitude, an attitude of relentless good will for the person in question, an attitude of doing what's right for another, an attitude of giving without regret or expectation to get rewarded, and a feeling which is understanding of truth and masterfully corrects falsehood. Without looking at Jesus, we would not be able to show or experience this kind of true love, God's love (Agape love).

Life has countless aspects like love that we all see and enjoy. Life has the material plane which gives us joy from all our senses, but it is not just joy or satisfaction that makes living worthwhile. Our excitement is triggered by things we like, but we all have experienced times when we were frighten or fearful for our lives to some degree, like when we get into a car accident, or a rattler snake appears on the sidewalk in front of you. There is an idea out there that people are not really scared of death, but that they are scared of the pain or very uncomfortable feelings associated with death. This idea might be right and there are people who have no fear of death, but if it all came down to it fear of death is a reflex that keeps us alive in times of danger, or can be the cause of our in action which makes us dead. Both ways, there is a fear of death, and as far as I know there is no one that has a fear of living. Some people might not like to be alive due to major hardship or pain of living, but they don't fear life. What I am trying to show you is that all people have a deep desire in their heart to want to live, not die.

You can believe that life is worth living, and worth living even more with Jesus. But, if for some reason you think that life is too hard or should be lived by going crazy with sin, then you can do that because you have a free will. There are consequences if you decide on the road Adam and Eve took, the only difference is that the life you will be choosing is an eternal life in hell, not a fallen world, and not heaven. People might think well this is an ultimatum, and yes it is; you can choose to accept life and salvation from a fallen world, or you can accept death and damnation by falling with the world. God has given free choice, but He prefers you choice salvation, not eternal death. Just like a parent would prefer the children to choose good things in life, instead of the bad things in life.

Chapter Fifteen

ॐ ----- ॐ

God Loves You!

God knew from the very beginning that He would have to die in your place in order to keep you in right standing with Him forever. God knew that Adam would sin and allow Eve to sin, even though they were like God and sinless. Why did God allow Adam and Eve to sin, well there are several reasons. The first one is that God has given you the ability to exercise your free will. God gave you free will so you would be able to know God's full extent of His love and have a relationship which He wants with you. If you didn't have free will, you would be nothing more than a robot in human flesh and react to a push of a button or how this generation would say, voice command. The other reason is simple logic. Adam and Eve were perfect in the sense that they were sinless and there was no internal sin working inside of them. The external influence of sin was Satan, but imagine if God would have said; Adam and Eve, both of you will die because of your sin, because I have to punish your sin, but the babies that you bare will be born sinless, but once they sin they will also be condemned to death. The babies that they bore will start fresh, but not in the Garden of Eden, but in a cursed Earth with sin all around them. They will be born and raised by already condemned sinners. What does that mean, it means that each person will be judged on their own merits, so technically a person might be able to grow up to be sinless until God decides to allow them to leave the cursed Earth and go to heaven without dying. There might be a very slim chance that someone will not be condemned to death. I say slim because if Adam and Eve were perfect and yet sinned how much easier will it be for anyone else to sin in a world full of sin?

Many people do not realize how much God loves them until they lose someone close to them. The problem is that they are center minded on their loss, which is normal, and most of the time want justice in the form of revenge, a comforting reason, a justified reason, or someone to blame. Once the initial pain is overcome, or maybe there is still pain, but not as much as before, the person looks either at God for comfort or turns his/her back towards God. This is a common reaction by small children even though they love you so much. A child might turn his/her back to you if you don't give them their favorite toy to play with or food to eat, or if they are simply mad at you for whatever reason. They pout and in time they will listen to your convincing apology or work around to get them to smile again. We remember the pain of loss deep inside of us the more we love that person. If we see a person who we might know, the pain of their death is there and we might feel bad about the situation, but we don't feel the agony of losing a child, parent, spouse, or grandparent. The situation of the death also makes things more intense. If a grandparent dies due to old age or better known as a long term illness with the expectation and preparation of death as part of life, then the grieving process is better managed by the loved ones. If the death is sudden let's say due to a suicide of a teen, then the impact of the lost is much more felt by the entire family in a stronger personal manner because someone in the family if not all may blame themselves for the suicide. If the death occurs due to a car accident then it can be more personal if the father or mother blames themselves for the accident, if they were driving. However, if the accident was not related to the parents, then the pain is there, but not as much or at the very least the blame is directed somewhere else (maybe the drunk driver in the other car). Now, imagine that you have a saintly daughter or sister who is drug free, a virgin, a wonderful person to be with. She is so wonderful and you are so proud to call her your sister or daughter. She is sixteen years old, and out of the darkness she is accused of witchcraft, and is sentenced to death by fire. The country which you are in is not your own country but a country you and your daughter decided to travel to. In a matter of hours your daughter is accused, sentenced, and burned alive at the stake. No one will listen to her or you in her defense. The reason she was accused of witchcraft was because she helped out a person to get better with medicine you had from the country you came from. During her punishment with great torturing pain, she asks you to forgive these people because they do not know what they do out of ignorance. She was innocent and in your heart you want to kill every person in this foreign country from the littlest to the oldest. The agony you feel is not going to be forgotten, and you will demand justice. Salvation is not in your plan for anyone at this point.

God loved you so much that He made a plan to save everyone before you were born, and it included showing you how much He loved you. God made it so everyone can receive salvation by sin passing through the seed of the man. If you are born a sinner, you will not need to work your way by not sinning in a world of sin. In fact your chances of getting to heaven are 100% in the fact that Jesus was that one person who did live a sinless life as a flesh and blood human for you. The seed of the woman is what matters in your salvation, because the seed of the woman is where Jesus was able to be born in the flesh without being tainted by the seed of the man. From the start, God prophesized His Son's death and victory over death, sin, and Satan in Genesis 3:15, "And I will put enmity between you (Satan) and the woman, and between your (Satan's) seed and her seed; He (Jesus) shall crush you (Satan) on the head, and you (Satan) shall bruise Him (Jesus) on the heel." That is what happened on the cross; the bruise on Jesus was Him dying even though He did not deserve to die. Satan lost his power over us and the world when his head was crushed by what Jesus did on the cross. Jesus took all humiliation before the cross, by being spat on by everyone in the garrison, being naked, being beaten and slashed to almost near death; so that we can stand before God without humiliation. Jesus had to carry his own instrument of punishment (the cross) to the mount where he was publicly displayed as a criminal, God allowed the Romans to put a crown of thorns on Jesus' head so He would take the curse which we and the Earth suffered from, giving us peace starting from the head down. Jesus became poor when His clothes were gambled away by the Soldiers at the foot of the cross, so that we would be rich. Sin was nailed on the cross through Jesus' hands and feet, so that we would not have to work to put sin behind us. Jesus' blood took our punishment and Jesus cried out in Mark 15:34 "My God, My God, why hast thou forsaken Me? (NASB, 1990)", so we would be able to say, "My Father, My God, why have you so blessed me."

God so loved you that He allowed His Son, Jesus, to die for you. Jesus was innocent, but yet He asked His Father to forgive the men that were crucifying Him. What kind of love allows pain to be suffered onto oneself so that others may not feel the agony of hell? John 3:16 says, "For God so loved the world, that He gave His only begotten Son, that whoever believes in Him should not perish, but have eternal life (NASB, 1990)." Jesus gave us an idea of the love of God by a story which many people think talks about a son (the prodigal son), but it is not. In the gospel of Luke 15:11, Jesus starts off the story with, "A certain man had two sons (NASB, 1990);" which indicates that the story is about this certain man, and as you keep reading, the two sons are the supporting characters. The father was rejected by the young son, but still waited and looked for his return, even though the law at that time was to have the younger son stoned to death by the elders of the town for his disrespect of the father. The younger son also did not return because he missed his father, he only returned because he was hungry and knew he would get feed three square meals a day like the servants of his father's house were feed. The younger son rehearsed what he would tell his father in order to get on his good side and become a servant. But the father never allowed the younger son to ask him to become his servant. In Luke 15:21-23 Jesus said, "And the son said to him, Father, I have sinned against heaven and in your sight; I am no longer worthy to be called your son. But the Father said to his servants, Quickly bring out the best robe and put it on him, and put the ring on his hand and sandals on his feet; and bring the fattened calf, kill it, and let us eat and be merry (NASB, 1990)." All this happened after the father saw the son from far away, sprinted out to embrace him and kiss him over and over because the father had great joy, all because he loved his son so much.

God's love as a father is one who sprints to you, embraces you with multiple kisses, gives you a robe of righteousness, gives you His ring of sonship, gives you the sandals of peace and prosperity, and most importantly He gives you Himself for all eternity. What more can you really want? The creator of the universe wants you to experience a life we can only imagine as beyond magnificent, but yet we look at all the paint on the wall (the world) and think that this is all there is and that no one loves me the way I want them to. There are people out there right now, suffering and suffering because of what Satan did from the beginning, now we can blame ourselves or someone else, that will not change your situation, but Jesus' presence inside of you will. Many people don't see this love from parents, who don't hug them, but instead hit them, physically or emotionally with anger. People don't see the love of God when we cry out for it, but instead get back rejection from another person, get robbed of our self esteem, get attacked emotionally or physically, get told we are not worth loving. This is what the religious people tell us.

To make things clear, the religious people are those who put a system of tradition to include science in front of you and tell you that this is the way life is or this is the way you have to live to be loved. The non-religious people are the people who do not claim a set of rules or mystical entities to provide a better way of life, they are the people who proclaim God's Son (His person) and His love which has saved us from eternal death. What do we live for is the question on the title of this book. Are you living for yourself, are you living just to live, are you living for this world, or are you living for Jesus and His love. All things work together for good, whether we think so or not. God is in control and His love is always faithful and just. There are probably many people who think that God's love ignores those children who were murdered, the good man who never heard of Jesus, but died suddenly and tragically, or the women who poured her love into a man who only tortured her and killed her for not making the perfect meal. God will have his justice, and His love will prevail. The blood Jesus gave for us will not allow those innocent people to go to hell. The only thing that will send someone to eternal damnation is rejecting/ignoring/defying God's personal salvation through His Son, Christ Jesus our Lord and Savior.

If you feel God speaking to you in your heart or mind, you don't have to do a good deed, or be forgiven to ask Jesus to be your Lord and Savior. If you understand or accept what has been said in this book about Jesus, ask Him now to come into your heart. Speak with your mouth and tell Him that you confess your sins from your heart, and believe that Jesus is the Son of God who died for my sins, took all my punishment for all time even until death on the cross, was raised from the dead by God, is now seated at the right hand of the Father making you an adopted child of God who has eternal life in Jesus. Amen.

If God just confirmed His salvation to you in your heart, do not doubt it and go find a church which is bible and Jesus focused. Find someone you can learn from, who teaches about Jesus. I highly recommend Joseph Prince, Joel Osteen, Chuck Swindoll, or Charles Stanley in that order. because they look at the bible as the reference and speak of Jesus, and God who loves you. These ministers are grace and bible based, not law and judgment based which according to Jesus is mixture and only teaches you bad doctrine. You should not feel beaten down in a church or by other people. You will know you are in the right place when the peace of Jesus is felt in your mind and heart. Once you find a church or a connection to what Jesus reveals to you, rest in Him. May you be edified and blessed by His presence. Amen.

Author Notes

ॐ ----- ॐ

I have studied and experienced many things before I gave my life to our Lord Christ Jesus. I was living it up watching the paint on the wall thinking it was true life. I was raised in a non-practicing family church environment, even though my parents were Roman Catholic. I was very disciplined and organized. It was I who did all the chores in the house even though I had a younger sister and older brother. I was not selfish, but I was self centered. I was not an 'A' student until the seventh grade, and I was very athletic, running a five minute mile at the age of 16. I would swim or play tennis after school maybe four to five times a week. I went to college at the age of 16, and had a very bright future. My family was not rich, but we were well off enough to have a roof over our heads and food on the table. I went into the US Army at the age of 17 to become an Airborne Ranger. At this point, I was truly egotistical and agnostic but also had great plans in taking over the world in order to make it a better place. I saw the life as a Ranger, and decided it was not for me. I ended up in light infantry, mechanized and airborne units for the next six years. After serving six years as an infantryman I got out of the Army, and that was when God humbled me. I gave my life to Jesus and finished my college BA degree in General Studies with a minor in Psychology. I was going to attend seminary, but went back into the US Army and later became a military counterintelligence officer. I retired as a Major in the US Army, with fourteen years overseas one year in Hawaii, and the rest was mostly in South Korea. I am married, have a daughter and two sons all over the age of 18.

I have personal experience in more than one debt crisis, alcoholism, family issues to include drugs, a rebellious teenager, and a few more dealing with work as a leader and professional Soldier. I am not saying I have done or seen it all, but I am not ignorant to many problems that the average person can go through. I have been in a position to see many people go through many problems, and unfortunately I was not able to help them all, the way I would have liked, but my point is we all go through many problems in our life time, but it doesn't have to be on the terms of the world or us, it can be on God's terms which is far better for yourself and everyone around you.

I have written two science-fiction novels, "Creator, A Superhero Epic (2004)" and "He is Known as Ego, A Superhero Epic (2006)". I am writing another book along with this one called, "North Korea for Dummies". I plan to write about the end of times. This is an interest to me because many people talk or write about the second coming or the end of the world, but I am not satisfied by the explanations on the biblical accounts, reasoning behind them, and why or how it all applies to our lives now. Jesus said not to worry about tomorrow, but He didn't say not to be ignorant of the future. Jesus tells us to look at the future, and witness of Him until He returns. It is interesting to note that when the disciples asked Jesus if He could tell them when Jesus was going to return. Jesus replied with things that must happen first before they see Him again. Jesus told them what not to do, which is in chapter 24 of Mathew. This account happened before His crucifixion and for some reason the disciples did not think that Jesus would have to leave them in order to return. Maybe the disciples though that Jesus would go back up to heaven like Elijah and return later, but if I were a disciple I would be asking Master, why must you leave us, why can't you just fix everything now?

The plan was there from the beginning and the plan is still there now for the second coming. We just need to focus on Jesus and let Him guide us in our lives. So does it really matter if we know the details of revelation? Maybe, but how much does it matter in the scheme of your life now? Well if you are worried about the future and focus on judgment coming upon you, then the book might help to alleviate some anxiety.

May this book continue to be a great blessing to you and your loved ones, by the knowledge of Christ Jesus, our Lord and God.

Amen.

References

Bauscher, D. G. Rev. (2010). The original Aramaic New Testament in plain English, 6ᵗʰ edition. Lulu Publishing.

Dictionary.com. (2012). Unabridged based on the random house dictionary. Random House, Inc. Retrieved from http://dictionary.reference.com/browse/religion.

Lanza, R. & Berman, B. (May, 2009). The biocentric universe theory: Life creates time, space, and the cosmos itself. Discover magazine. Retrieved from http://discovermagazine.com/2009/may/01-the-biocentric-universe-life-creates-time-space-cosmos

Merriam-Webster. (2012). An encyclopedia Britannica company. Merriam-Webster, Inc. http://www.merriam-webster.com/dictionary/common%20sense.

NASB. (1990). The new American standard bible; open bible, study edition. Thomas Nelson, Inc. Nashville, TN.